MW01193504

Holy Smoke

Loose Herbs & Hot Embers for
INTENSE
Group Smudges & Smoke Prayers

by

Amy *"Moonlady"* Martin

Holy Smoke:
Loose Herbs & Hot Embers for
Intense
Group Smudges & Smoke Prayers

Copyright 2010 Amy Martin

published by

www.Moonlady.com

381 Casa Linda Plaza, box 137, Dallas, Texas 75218
moonladymedia@sbcglobal.net

SAN: 856-7026

All rights reserved. The written consent of Moonlady Media
is required to reproduce any part of this book,
including by photocopy or electronic text.

ISBN 10: 0-9818424-1-0
ISBN 13: 978-0-9818424-1-7

Library of Congress Control Number

First Printing August 2010

Printed in the United States of America

Table of Contents

And she forgot the stars, the moon, the sun,

And she forgot the blue above the trees,
And she forgot the dells, where waters run,
And she forgot the chilly autumn breeze;
She had no knowledge when day was done,
And the new morn she saw not: but in peace
Hung over her sweet Basil evermore...
'For cruel 'tis,' said she,
'To steal my Basil-pot away from me.'

– John Keats

Introduction

How These Techniques and Blends Came to Be

I am an herb junkie. As a pre-teen in the tamped-down WASP-nirvana that was Dallas in the '60s, I was totally enamored with the herbal shampoo from Clairol, a marketing nod to the era's hippies. To this day, if I see "herb" in a description at a restaurant I'll order the dish. All my soaps, shampoos and such have some aroma to them, and the first thing I do in my office in the morning is turn on the essential-oil diffuser.

It's worse than that. I buy herbs I'll never use, just because they're cool. How can you resist something named boldo? It's supposed to have quite a buzz, though I've never had the nerve to try it. I had small jars of High John the Conqueror and Jacob's ladder just because I like esoteric herbs with Biblical names. I finally had to cut back my herb hoarding to free up cabinet space for important things like food.

Though obsessed with herbs, I've never had the patience to make potions and lotions or to delve into their medicinal qualities. Instead I've explored the art of working with raw herbs, either burning them as loose herbs on hot embers, as outlined in this book, or strewing for sacred space and creating power potpourris, as covered in my book "Raw Herbs: Power Potpourris for Mood Enhancement & Strewing for Sacred Space."

Keep in mind that herbs encompass so much more than leafy green plants like the oregano in your marinara sauce. In this book, herbs include seeds, flowers and even roots, plus wood, bark and resin from trees. Everything you need to know about buying and working with herbs is in the **Herbal 101** chapter.

Who Am I?

The recipes and knowledge in this book come from leading rituals and ceremonies in North Texas for nearly 20 years. My flagship event is Winter SolstiCelebration, going strong each December since 1993 and now attended by more than 1,000 folks. However, most of these herbal techniques for smudging and strewing were developed at warmer, outdoor events. My title is Executive Director of the non-profit Earth Rhythms (www.EarthRhythms.org), but I greatly prefer the term "Poohbah."

My other moniker is the "Moonlady" (www.moonlady.com), a name that arose from being born on a Full Moon and a propensity for howling. Email promotions for my seasonal events eventually spun off a list serve called Moonlady News, with 3,200+ members at last count. It networks North Texas events and activities that are spiritual, holistic, metaphysical, progressive or simply eclectic. My husband, Scooter Smith, and I operate Moonlady Media, which publishes books and other products.

Necessity Is the Mother of Invention

As my seasonal events grew more popular, it became laborious to smudge so many people. I'd watch the energy of the circle deflate as folks stood around bored and waiting for the smudge stick to go around. So I began using loose herbs on a hibachi of hot charcoal to create billows of aromatic smoke. This way a half-dozen or more people could be smudged in just a few seconds, not with just a light smoke blessing, but with a thorough, aura-cleansing smoke bath that swept stress away.

People responded deeply to the fiery, sharp aroma and immediate impact of my first purification blend based on sage and yerba santa, but it only made folks want more. The next blend was a luscious smudge with mugwort and myrrh that corresponded with the Moon. Smudges especially for men, women and seasonal bonfire rituals soon followed.

With perfect embers so easily at hand, the lost art of burnt offerings was resurrected, this time with herbs instead of animal flesh. A pinch of herbs held in the hand was infused with intent or prayers, and then placed on embers to create a smoky conduit to the divine.

I developed herb smoke-prayer blends to address human needs like releasing negative patterns, attracting love, and honoring the passage of loved ones, plus psychological needs such as lifting depression, creating deep trance and meditative states, inspiring vivid dreams and raising libidos. Ritual blends were created to celebrate nature's archetypes such as the Sun, Moon and World Tree.

It was a vigorous but fun learning curve. I came to understand how to tweak the herb recipes so that the aromas were pleasing – some early blends were literal stinkers! I figured out how to balance the resins, woods and leaves so that blends burned easily and smoothly, unfolding their aromas over time.

Gratitude

I am grateful to the members of the Moonlady Community in North Texas for their energy and support, and to the many hundreds of people who have attended my seasonal events and been the test subjects for many of these blends. I am also grateful to the women of the Goddess Creative and Women's Well listserves for their encouragement of my writing. But most of all I am grateful to my husband Scooter Smith for his support and impeccable work designing and laying out this book.

How to Use this Book

This book was written for people who want to work with herbs, particularly in groups, but want to keep it simple. It's like a recipe book. Look up what you want to do, make a shopping list and go to the store or website. Then simply prepare and enjoy the blends. No cooking required!

- The book's first section features an essay on smoke, plus everything you need to know for creating perfect embers to burn herbs.
- The two central sections showcase recipes and techniques for creating and using smudges and smoke prayers.
- The following section details suggestions on how to use smudges and smoke prayers in various kinds of rituals and ceremonies.
- The concluding section contains a brief primer on working with herbs and a glossary of herbs used in the recipes.

I take great pleasure in working with herbs and want to share some of that with you. Let these recipes be a starting point in your own exploration of burning herbs. Feel free to experiment and develop new blends. May the knowledge in this book bring you the same joy it has bought me!

Ceremony & Circle Leaders
Holy Smoke for Memorable Events

As a fellow ceremony leader, this book was written with you in mind. We are constantly being challenged to find new ways to present rituals. We encounter circles and groups whose energy is unfocused, chaotic or low. We have members who struggle with their evolution and we want to help them break through that impasse. We seek things that set sabbat gatherings apart from the usual weekly or monthly circles.

Immersion smudges and burnt offerings should become part of your repertoire of ritual tools. Nothing activates the mind like our sense of smell. Clouds of wildly aromatic smoke and warm fires insure your participants have a vivid and highly memorable sense-filled experience. Immersion smudges and burnt offerings or smoke prayers require active engagement from those gathered, negating the tendency to passively go along.

Festivals can get rowdy, especially weekend-long camping ones where people gather from across a region. You can absolutely manage a crowd with a deft use of bonfire embers and loose herbs – sober them up, chill them out and take them places mentally. This is powerful stuff!

Groups that have a weekly or monthly circle will find the creation of these herbal blends to be a great communal activity and a hands-on way to learn about ceremonial herbs. You can pool resources and buy the herbs in bulk online at low cost. Make enough for everyone to take some home.

For deep transformational rituals that require no elaborate instructions or memorized scripts, immersion smudges and burnt offerings are at the top! Specific suggestions are in the **Smoke-Based Ceremonies** section.

Disclaimers

A Dose of Common Sense

Here's the part where I tell you things that are simple common sense.

Disclaimer #1: **Use common sense.**

This book assumes you have some. The author cannot be held liable for your lack of common sense.

Disclaimer #2: **Don't burn yourself up.**

The burning techniques outlined in this book incorporate bonfires, charcoal, lighter fluid and butane lighters. Exercise caution when working with flammable stuff. Read and follow all cautions detailed in the book.

Disclaimer #3: **Don't burn everybody else up.**

It's easy to get carried away. You are responsible for the safety of others.

Disclaimer #4: **Keep your head on.**

Inhaling the smoke of some herbal blends described in this book may impair judgment. They are noted as such in the text. After ingesting these blends, do not drive vehicles, perform complex tasks or operate large machinery. Just chill. All cautions mentioned in the book must be read and obeyed.

Disclaimer #5: **Bad lungs stay away.**

If you have respiratory issues, do not get near the fumes of charcoal while it is being ignited nor inhale the smoke of burning herbs. Asthma attacks put a damper on festivities.

Smoke

Elements & Archetypes in Action

Perhaps I am just easily amused, but I have spent hours over a hibachi of hot charcoal and jars of herbs, sprinkling one herb after another on the embers and watching the smoke rise. The different herbs and resins produced a plethora of smoke personalities – swirling or soaring, thick or wispy, white or grey, vigorous or relaxed. The aromas lingered and wove together in an ethereal tapestry.

As the burning herbs surrounded me with their aromatic dance, one thing became obvious. The seemingly still and empty air was seething with motion. Smoke makes the invisible manifest. It was obvious that the air was alive, not just the aerobic sweep of breezes, but a plentitude of small currents, eddies and doldrums, each leaf, each branch, each garden wall or archway creating microcosms of weather to which the smoke responded.

If connection with all things was something I could feel in transcendental moments, here it was revealed to me visually through the medium of smoke. One night I put a large chunk of myrrh, a tree resin, on the embers. Thick white clouds of smoke roiled out of the hibachi and down, then caught a current and spiraled upward. The myrrh unfolded wave after wave of sweet heavy smoke until all separation between the tangible world and I was blurred and there was only oneness. The smoke lifted and opened to the breeze before dissipating into nothing but aroma.

A Smoky History

Years later, I visited the Yucatan area of Mexico in search of sacred sites of the Mayan goddess Ix Chel (ee shell). At Mayan ceremonies there, copious quantities of the tree resin copal are burned on bonfire embers, frequently in caves or under shelters, forming an intense sauna of smoke that leaves everyone red-eyed and coughing, yet blessed by the baptismal experience. Copal smoke holds and intensifies spiritual energy, causing everything within it to glow with a vibrant peace, going beyond purification to a total communion with the divine – meeting spirit in the ether where it lives.

The ritual burning of herbs goes far before and beyond the Native American smudge stick and Mayan ceremonies. Rare is the Buddhist, Hindu, Shinto or Taoist temple without ample incense burning at all times. Catholics are familiar with the aromatic smoke spilling from the priest's swinging thurible. In ancient Egypt, the burning of frankincense at noon to honor Sun deities was perhaps the world's first formal smoke ritual.

Personalities of Smoke

In my smoky ruminations around the hibachi, fiery white sage shot intensely upward with a pure white smoke, while mugwort, herb of the moon, circulated low and lazy before rising, reflecting their lunar and solar natures. Thin leaves like basil fumed a brief aroma burst of dancing white smoke, while the fuzzy leaves of coltsfoot simmered on the embers to slowly release a soft vanilla waft. Few flowers have the substance to burn well, but chamomile was surprisingly aromatic with a fine wispy smoke. Seeds and berries, so potently concentrated, sizzled and then popped in unexpected aroma bombs.

Wood chips and bark shreds were a revelation on the embers. Igniting slowly, the substantial thick grey smoke spread out and barely drifted upward, and the tree aromas unfurled lazily. To smell sandalwood in its raw form is vastly different from incense. Fuzzy slippery elm bark burned with a root beer aroma.

Mysterious and uber-powerful roots ignited obstinately, slowly unveiling layers of smell as the dense material baked and smoldered. Wild lettuce root burned with a crazy swirling smoke and an absolutely unique aroma that was oddly compelling. The ginger aroma of galangal root leapt out at you, while calamus' spiceness was pervasive but subtle.

The richest, most aromatic smoke arises from burning tree resins, the very essence, or blood, of the tree. Sap rising and falling over the course of the year is the rhythm of the forest. The sticky sap of sacred trees, most often from desert regions, is concentrated and dried into amber-like chunks of resin. Rich with natural hydrocarbons, resins burn easily and leisurely, flaming with passion when the embers are too hot, giving richly of themselves with aromas that seize the mind.

A Sensual Elemental Experience

Pulsing red embers radiate the potential of fire. Into the smoldering heat is placed the concentrated product of earth – leaf, flower, seed, root, resin and bark – transforming into smoke and steam that infuse into the air. Mix with that each herb's own elemental leanings – the fire of frankincense, the water of calamus, the earth of patchouli, the air of acacia – and the archetypes of elements come vividly alive through burning herbs.

Immersion smudging and smoke prayers take ritual beyond rote words and action by embracing the warm feel of the fire, the delicate touch of smoke on the skin, the visual delight of fire and fumes and, most of all, the invigorating sense of smell with its immediate and lively effect on mind and memory. These are the embodied moments that people can remember and call upon in their times of need. All you need is the knowledge contained in this book to create them.

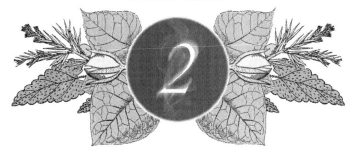

The Art of Embers
Fire Making for Herb Burning

An ember is concentrated passion. The mighty tree has so much energy that it can resurrect itself, burning once as wood and then, after the dancing flames have died down, continuing in ember form. The heat of quietly smoldering red coals can rival that of the flames it took to create them. Embers are the seed of fire ready to come alive, but willing to wait, their incredible elemental power now tamed to be of service for us.

Indoor Burning

Toasty hot embers from barbeque charcoal are required for burning these herb blends, especially when a lot of smudge smoke is desired. The familiar little self-lighting charcoal discs used for incense are just too wimpy to produce volumes of smoke out of anything except finely ground tree resins. Believe me, I've tried. Once a drought-induced burn ban prohibited open fires at a retreat where I was leading a smudge ritual. The sight of us huddled around a small cast-iron cauldron, trying to get a couple dozen incense-charcoal discs to burn the herbal blends was pitiful. A cigarette would have made more smoke.

However, if a Native American style smoke blessing or extremely light smudge is your thing, many of the herbal blends will work sans barbeque charcoal.

Incense Charcoal Discs	Most of the blends will burn on the little self-lighting charcoal rounds if they are ground very fine and several discs used at once. Blends with a lot of woods and roots will be the most difficult to burn.
Shell Burning	If planning to go sans charcoal disc and simply burn herbs in a shell or other fireproof container, blends that are mostly leaves or flowers will work. Recipes with woods, roots or resins need much higher heat to ignite than a lighter can provide..
Direct Burning	When you need a super-fast smoke prayer or slight smudge, nothing beats white sage tips. Burning the entire tight bundle of leaves at the end of Salvia apina plant lights quickly and produces a surprising amount of smoke very fast, enough for a brief smudge. Agarwood, also called aloeswood, is a sacred wood of Asia that is scarce and expensive, so it is often burned directly as wood chips. The slightly evergreen and floral aroma is extremely centering and jolts you immediately out of daydreams or worry into present time.

Bonfires & Fireplace Fires

Wood stacked and set fire will crack and shatter, falling downward to form an ever increasing pile of embers. These are perfect for herb burning and are conveniently kept warm by the flames above. Just scoop some out with a long-handled metal tool like a garden shovel.

Carefully move the embers to the edge of the fire pit or place in a fire container. A hibachi holds just the right amount of embers at a good height and size for smudging. A large enough shovel, like those for moving manure or snow, can serve as an impromptu ember holder. Fire containers covered in more detail later in the chapter.

Types of Charcoal

Barbeque charcoal is a fast and dependable way to achieve hot embers. Charcoal is made by slowly burning wood or other carbohydrate-rich material in a low-oxygen environment, similar to a ceramics kiln. Stuff like hydrogen, oxygen and nitrogen burns away, while leaving the sturdy carbon intact. The result is similar to coal: soft, lightweight, porous chunks of smudgy black material that lights easily.

It once was easy to dismiss charcoal as too messy or an environmental nightmare. Now sources for charcoal include environmentally harvested wood and lumber industry waste. Plant-sourced ethanol lighter fluid is easily available. In addition, you can get it all in an affordable one-use bag of eco-charcoal. You simply light the bag and come back in a half-hour to a pile of perfect embers.

Lump Charcoal vs Natural Charcoal

Old-timey charcoal is called lump charcoal or char wood and is made directly from trees. It burns at just the right temperature for all types of herbs and lasts a long time. However, it's an awful waste of forest! Look around in stores and check online for increasingly available eco-options. The Rainforest Alliance's SmartWood program will certify char wood made from ecologically harvested wood. Some brands are made from trees like mesquite and cedar that can be aggressive invaders of ecosystems and are best removed.

The best choice is natural charcoal derived from wood products left over from timber and lumber industry processing. Very environmentally sound! It's easy to find in eco or health food stores and is gaining wider distribution. The recycled timber pieces are often flat, which holds the burning herbs better, and it's generally cheap, but very bulky. It goes to embers fast and burns out quick. Because most natural charcoal burns cooler than charwood or briquettes, use more of it when burning blends that are heavy on roots and woods.

Charcoal Briquettes

Charcoal briquettes are made by pressing wood waste and sawdust into lumps with an industrial binder, usually plant starch, and then charring, though occasionally the source material is charred before pressing. The recycling part is cool, but in cheap briquettes the binders can be made from industrial weirdness; ones that are more expensive use food-grade binder.

All charcoal briquettes have a crap-to-carbon ratio. The crap includes the binder, plus ash from charring. Fairly innocuous limestone may be added so the coals acquire a white coating when ready. Nasty fire accelerants like nitrate and coal dust are sometimes included. The preferred crap-to-carbon ratio in briquettes is more than 80% carbon, but cheap ones can be as little as half carbon. The FDA does not require that charcoal ingredients be listed on the label, so you are best sticking with more expensive brands.

Briquettes have a unique mix of qualities. They are compact and easy to store. The briquettes stand up to cold temperatures well and last a long time, but they also take quite a while to cool down to proper embers. Herbs tend to slide off the curved briquettes unless the embers are crushed.

Coming on strong are binder-free briquettes that are made by extruding wood waste, coconut shells and other carbohydrate matter under intense pressure into shapes that are charred. Sometimes the source material is pre-charred. Extrusion briquettes burn hotter and last longer than regular briquettes, natural charcoal or char wood. Their crap-to-carbon ratio is around 95% carbon.

Self-lighting briquettes are saturated with petrochemical lighter fluid, making them super easy to ignite. Build a pyramid of briquettes in a container, light it and come back in 20 minutes to hot coals. They are also a bad environmental offender, with loads of petro-fumes during the flame up period. Some jurisdictions ban their use. A faint petro smell will remain in the embers. Toss cedar shavings on during ignition and early ember stages to take the chemical edge off.

Insta-Light Charcoal Bags

The best of all worlds is charcoal pre-packed in a one-use bag. Simply light the bag and it burns away, igniting the charcoal in the process. Unlike self-lighting briquettes, most insta-bags do not set up much of a stink when ignited. Absolutely no mess or stink from handling smudgy charcoal or lighter fluid – this is a big plus.

Traditional briquette insta-light bags can be found at most any grocery store and natural charcoal ones at eco and health-food stores. They are surprisingly affordable and just the right size for a hibachi. The bags make it very easy to do charcoal smudging rituals in remote places by reducing the amount of stuff to schlep.

You can also use them to start a larger fire by layering on additional natural charcoal once the bag is fully aflame. The end result is a blend of embers at the perfect temperature, yet lasts a long time.

Igniting the Fire or Charcoal

Lighters

You need to keep at least 6 inches be-
tween your hand and the material you're igniting, especially self-lighting briquettes which tend to flame up fast. So a long wand lighter, also called a utility or candle lighter, is necessary. Some pagans term it a "Sacred Bic."

wand lighters

Candle lighters are usually disposable one-use deals, though refillable butane styles can be found. Some can look quite elegant. Wind-resistant versions are available. Online tobacco stores have an excellent selection of lighters.

Non-petroleum ignition alternatives include hemp wick and long fireplace matches. Hemp wick is hemp twine impregnated with a natural wax. Cut small strips off, light and lay upon the charcoal. Or make a torch by wrapping the hemp wick around the end of a long stick.

Lighter Fluid

The easy way to light charcoal or firewood is with lighter fluid. A preferred ignition accelerant is non-petroleum lighter gel made from ethanol, the same corn-sourced product that's often blended into gasoline. Similar to canned heat, often called Sterno, the gel is odorless and smokeless. No fumes!

Eco-Start

Conventional charcoal lighter fluid and accelerant for self-lighting charcoal are made from kerosene. Using them creates so much smog-causing petroleum pollution that the products are banned in many places. If you must use petro lighter fluid, choose a double-filtered "odorless" version and apply sparingly. To lessen petro fumes, wait for the lighter fluid to soak in for a minute before igniting.

~~~

Wood Fires

Making a camp fire or bonfire that lights easily and lasts long is a true skill. It's also a skill that I don't have. But it seems to key around two things:

1) Build a small fire to light a big one. Lay down a tinder bed of highly flammable materials like shredded paper, tiny sticks or dried leaves. On top of that place lots of small and medium sticks for kindling. Don't skimp on the kindling and make sure it's very dry. Stack the firewood on the kindling and light the tinder in several places. You can cheat by forgoing the tinder and coating the kindling with ethanol lighter gel, or integrating "fat wood" easy-lighting sticks. Daub a little more gel on the firewood as well.

2) Fire needs air circulation. Stack the firewood so that a chimney is formed in the middle, drawing up air. If the fire is slow to get going, carefully fan it with a stiff flat object or, better yet, use a fireplace bellows that shoots out a focused blast of air. A few gusts on embers will cause them to flame up, as Smoky the Bear will sadly attest.

If you've got one handy, turn to a current or former Boy or Girl Scout for a lesson in fire making and tending. Many of these folks have been trained to make fires in a variety of conditions. Barbeque lovers can also be good teachers, as long as they haven't gone soft from using gas units.

Charcoal Fires

Pour about a half-gallon jug amount of charcoal in the hibachi. Daub on ethanol lighter gel and thoroughly mix, or lightly douse with petro lighter fluid if you absolutely have no other option. Stir charcoal and form into a pyramid. The shape aids in air flow while containing the heat. Light the pile using a long-handled device. A fair amount of flames will shoot up for a few minutes. After the initial fire has died down embers will begin to form.

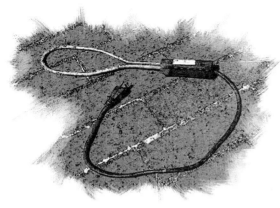
electric charcoal starter

Or go sans accelerant by igniting charcoal in separate charcoal starter or charcoal chimney, basically a large metal can with holes in the bottom and a handle on the side. Line the bottom with crumbled newspaper or tinder, fill with charcoal and light it from the bottom. The starter will put out a lot of smoke from the tinder at first, but no flames, allowing you to ignite charcoal when there's a ban on open flames.

Another flame-free option is an electric charcoal starter. Insert the long metal wand into a starter or chimney and pack charcoal loosely around it. Plug in and wait about 10 minutes until charcoal is glowing. But don't forget and leave it for too long or any plastic in the starter handle will melt, which I learned the hard way.

Charcoal chimneys and electric starters can be found at many home improvement and department stores.

Once the embers have attained a state of heat perfection, spread the charcoal to create a level surface. Smoosh the embers to create lots of hot surface area with an even bed.

Fire Containers for Groups

Hibachis

Weber Smoky Joe

Hibachi is the Japanese word for "fire bowl." The quintessential apartment balcony barbeque grill, a classic round hibachi is perfect for burning herbs. My favorite is the Smokey Joe line from Weber [www.weber.com]. This squatty lightweight black porcelain-enameled steel hibachi is about 17 inches tall and 15 inches across.

Weber One Touch

The round bowl has air-intake holes in the bottom that allows accumulated ash to drop out. It does get very hot, but cools off fast. The lid has adjustable vent holes. Put it on the hibachi with the holes partly closed to preserve hot embers between uses.

Smokey Joe is great for smudging because it small and low, so you can get up close. Straddle the hibachi to smudge the goods! It also has a tripod leg system, which evokes the classic cauldron. The larger One-Touch Silver line sits about a yard high and two of the legs have wheels for easy moving. It's good for offerings, but not smudges. Either of these hibachis will run you $30 to $40 new.

Hibachis can be found at many home improvement and department stores. Stay away from cheap rectangular hibachis often sold in department stores. The design is too shallow to handle charcoal well. They're usually made of aluminum and don't stand up to regular use.

Cast-iron has the advantage of being very stable and attractive, and the disadvantage of being heavy to carry and slow to cool. For the best in cast-iron units seek out the Sportsman's Grill by Lodge [www.lodgemfg.com] with its nice deep oval charcoal well and excellent air ventilation system. It's about 9 inches wide and 20 inches long. At only 8 inches high, it's a little low for herb burning, though that makes it nearly impossible to tip over. The cost is over $80, but a cast-iron unit will last forever.

Though hibachis were designed for charcoal, you can use them to hold embers from bonfires and fireplaces.

Fire Pits & Kettles

Portable metal fire pits work best for firewood, though charcoal can be used. Since they tend to be wide, getting close enough for a good immersion smudging can be a challenge. Kettles are taller and good for smoke prayers. Both usually have handy wheels. Expect to pay $100 or more for a quality one.

Chimeneas

A chimenea is an enclosed fire pit with a vertical chimney and an opening on the side to insert firewood. Most chimeneas are made of pottery, but occasionally metal ones can be found. Because the chimney directs the smoke upward, chimeneas are suitable for burnt offerings, but not for smudges.

Pottery

A terra cotta clay garden pot can serve as a charcoal-burning container as long as it's about 1/3 inch thick and unglazed. A wide and relatively shallow shape works best because it creates more hot surface area and allows for better air motion. The drainage hole facilitates some air intake if the pot is set on an elevated non-flammable grid. These pots will eventually crack from the heat and make a big mess, but are cheap to replace.

Fire Containers for Individuals & Indoor Use

Sometimes a smaller, more portable system is needed. The units described below can be used with modest amounts of barbeque charcoal and herbs to produce significantly more smoke than a smudge stick, but less than a hibachi.

cast iron censer

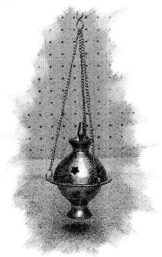

thurible

A censer is a metal or stone container for holding hot incense charcoal discs to burn resin incense. Censers can look really cool! When suspended from a chain, as typically seen in Catholic ceremonies, it's called a thurible. The suspending chain can get dang hot! Make sure you get a thurible that can stand erect when you set it down on a surface.

Indigenous Mesoamerican and Mayan ceremonies often feature a large terra cotta clay chalice that holds two to three cups or embers. These are porous enough to dissipate heat quickly and are cooler to hold. Such chalices range from simple to ornate. A miniature chimenea, usually about 10 inches high, is very similar and quite portable.

However, these units are too cramped to start barbeque charcoal in. It took a couple of ceremonial embarrassments before I figured that out. Instead, fill the unit with embers from a separate fire. The units can be used indoors for a brief smudging as long as no birds are present and the rooms are well ventilated afterward.

terra cotta chalice

Burning the Herbs

Depending on how much charcoal you used and the outside temperature, from igniting the fire to perfect embers, you can expect to wait 30 to 60 minutes. Embers cool down slower in hot weather and when in big piles.

Whether you create them from firewood or charcoal, the perfect ember for burning herbs is much less hot than what's required for cooking food. A white ash cover is often a signal that the ember is cool enough.

The sure test is applying a dusting of herbs. Does it cause flames to arise? If so, it's too hot; though highly flammable tree resins will often put up an initial flare. To cool down embers, toss on some dried organic matter to burn off some of the heat.

After several applications of herbs, stir and re-level the embers with a metal poker to keep them fresh and hot. If you start the herb burning just after the embers are ready, the charcoal will remain the right temperature for about 20 minutes.

Extinguishing Embers

After the embers have lost most of their heat, allow 30 to 60 minutes to cool down completely. The best way to extinguish hot embers is to let them to burn up completely so that only ash is left. Keep in mind that embers can be covered with ash and appear to be out, yet still be flammable. Stir well and check carefully. A blast of air is all that's need to spark a lukewarm ember into flames.

If you must leave before the embers are burned up, or just want to be sure they're out, douse with water. To keep from making a mess of the hibachi, turn the embers out onto bare dirt or pavement and then wet down.

Ember remains and ash from natural and extrusion charcoal may be scattered or composted. Briquette ember remains and ash should be disposed of with regular garbage.

Safety & Fire Tools

Don't use hibachis or make bonfires during drought conditions or when it's windy. Check to see if your county has decreed a ban on open fires due to unsafe conditions.

bellows and iron poker

There are a few things you must keep on hand when working with embers.

For fire maintaining:	A long metal rod or poker to stir and adjust the embers, though a thick stick will do in a pinch
	Hand bellows that pump to dispense a steady stream of air to encourage recalcitrant charcoal to ignite, or a wide and sturdy fan
	A pair of heat-resistant gloves, especially if your burner does not have handles
For fire safety:	A small fire extinguisher, especially if burning anywhere near dry grass and other tinder
	A gallon jug of water to extinguish the coals, if desired

Fire making can be messy. Bring pre-moistened wipes or soapy water and rags for clean up.

Cautions

fire extinguisher

Burning charcoal and wood produces soot particles and small amounts of carbon monoxide. Don't breathe the fumes of fires, especially if you have respiratory issues. Asthmatics and others with lung ailments should wear a respiratory dust mask.

Self-lighting charcoal and conventional lighter fluid use releases volatile organic compounds that contribute to air pollution. They are horrid for anyone to breathe.

dust mask

Be careful around embers if you're wearing long or flowing clothes. Human candles can really spoil a gathering.

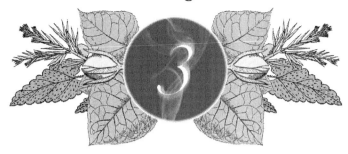

Taking a Smoke Bath
Industrial-Strength Smudges for Tough Times

If you're going to smudge, then really smudge – that's my motto and a theme of this book. I love Native American style smudge sticks and burning loose herbs in a shell, though I see that as more of a smoke blessing or prayer. If a thorough cleansing of the aura if what you want, using a smudge stick is like trying to lick yourself clean. By tossing loose herbs on hot embers, billows of aromatic smoke are created. It's a whole-body immersion-style smudge that Mayans have done for centuries.

Maintaining the Aural Body

Like most folks, I live in an urban locale. Crowded city streets and insanely congested highways are a daily bane. Exposure to cranky and negative people is the norm. Stress levels are high. Some of it is going to stick to you no matter what. After a while you start looking like the Pig Pen character from the Peanuts comic strip with a dingy cloud swirling about your body.

At the same time, our own frustrations and tension, worry and grief, get projected outward. That also ends up stuck in the aura. After a while it all becomes heavy baggage indeed. It's hard for your own internal spirit to shine through that haze.

Keep your aura clean just as you do your corporeal body. My ethereal body stays spiffy with one or more of these smudges a month:
- a 4th quarter smudge for releasing
- a New Moon smudge for initiating a process

- a Full Moon smudge for opening up
- Seasonal smudge

Whose Sage is This Anyway?

At a Moon circle one night, I breathed in the sharp aroma of my sage-based blend and watched the thin dry smoke rise in a direct vertical stream. It caused me to wonder if a sweet, circular and relaxed smoke would be more Moon evocative.

That got me to ruminating about the white sage used in smudges and how it's a Native American tradition. But I'm a BWG: Basic White Girl. So what would be a smudge from my genetic heritage?

Herbals from Yea Olde Europe list these as indigenous herbal purifiers:
- Leafy herbs like bay laurel, blue vervain, hyssop, rosemary and thyme
- Woods such as cedar, cypress and juniper
- Roots like calamus and valerian

Exotic imported resins such as frankincense and myrrh, and spices like cardamom and cinnamon, were also included.

One very big problem: Hardly any of that can be bound into a smudge stick — especially the resins and that's some of the best stuff!

Variety, Flexibility and Intimacy

To create a smudge stick, the leaves must remain attached to a sturdy stem; most herb leaves easily fall off. The oil content of the leaves has to be high enough so they stay pliable and stick together, plus they need to ignite easy and remain lit.

That cuts out most of the herbal lexicon! Why limit yourself? With loose herbs on hot embers you are free to use resin, wood, root, any kind of leaf, even flowers. With such variety available, a smudge blend can be fine tuned for any intent, any occasion and even any aroma!

A great synergy develops in the blends. Flammable resins help hard-to-ignite roots and spices to combust into smoke, while woods provide a long-lasting base that extends the quick burn of leaves. With the different burning speeds, waves of aromas arise from the embers, unfolding and blending into aerial potpourris.

When being smudged with a stick, I was always very aware of the person smudging me. The ceremonial interaction could be nice, but for me purification is a personal thing. In loose-leaf immersion smudges, the smudgee can do it all, adjusting the amount of smoke to their desire. It can be an exceedingly powerful and private moment, just the hot embers, herbs and a self in need.

How To & Tips

To do an immersion smudge, get your whole body into it. Lean over the smoke and smudge your chest and head. Remember your hands and feet, those parts of you that most often intersect with the world. Don't forget to smudge your butt and straddle the hibachi to smudge your private parts. To smudge a group at one time, have them stand downwind of the embers or use fans to direct the smoke.

Folks with sensitive skin should moisturize their face and exposed areas for protection before they begin. Those with lung issues should stand further from the smoke and consider using a respiratory dust filter mask.

Your clothes, skin and hair will absolutely reek of herbal smoke afterward. Sometimes the aroma is so strong it makes my cats sneeze. Simple airing of clothes won't do the trick; it usually takes washing to remove the aroma.

Getting Jiggy With It

So why not smudge sans clothing? That is an option! And an interesting one. Naked smudging allows some of the herbs' active ingredients to be absorbed into your skin, increasing their health benefits. For some smudges, the experience can be deepened by lightly inhaling the smoke. Blends in the book especially suitable for inhaling and sky-clad smudging are in the Specialized section.

If intending to inhale a smudge, always add the Lung Buffer herb blend into the herbs. This is important. Also stand far enough away from the source so that the smoke is cool enough to inhale. Do not inhale warm or hot smoke.

The cautions: Mind-altering herbs in the Specialized smudges are useful for trance and meditation. They are to be used only by adults in a private setting.

Partake gradually and at a slow pace so that you can judge your dose. These herbs are not for use by children or teens. They are not appropriate for anyone on psychiatric medication or for pregnant or nursing women. Do not drive or operate machinery on these herbs.

Step Into the Smoke

We wash our bodies in water, bake them in saunas and cover them with earth in masques. Why not complete the elemental excursion with a smoke bath! Smudges provide a supremely effective method to shift from the mundane to the sacred, to let go and release into the realm of potential.

Smudge Recipes

Welcome to the wild world of loose-herb smudges!

For the complete scoop of how to work with herbs, including details on purchase and storage, please see the chapter **Herbal 101**. But the crib notes below
will help you interpret the recipes.

Herb Basics

The recipes feature herbs as you would buy them from a store or web outlet. In
general, ground up versions will lose their potency faster than larger and more
intact pieces of herbs.

Essential oils	A few herbs such as clary sage are gener-ally available only as an essential oil. But essential oils don't fare so well on the high heat of charcoal.
Flowers	Flowers are sold as dried petals or com-plete blossoms.
Leaves	Leafy herbs are usually sold as dried leaves that have been cut into 1/2 inch or smaller pieces and sifted for stems. A few herbs like bay laurel are sold whole and then hand crushed.

Resins	Resins are usually sold in plastic-like masses ranging in size from small pearls to sizable chunks that are easy to crush. Some resins are sold as powders.
Roots	Roots are usually sold in small chunks of dried roots. They can be very hard! Unless you have a good sturdy grinder, buy powdered roots.
Woods	Woods are usually sold as small chunks or shavings.

Here are a few abbreviations used in the recipes:
- Tbsp for Tablespoon
- Tsp for Teaspoon
- C for Chunks
- P for Powdered
- W for Whole

Using the Blends

Basic designations of significant Moons, seasonal dates, holy days and ceremonial situations are listed for each herbal blend. More ideas on how to use the blends are in the section **Smoke-Based Ceremonies**.

Smudge Recipes

GENERAL	Feminine Focus
	Lunar Purification
	Masculine Manna
	Solar Purification

SEASONAL	Spring Equinox
	Beltane & Midsummer
	Summer Solstice
	Autumn Equinox
	Winter Solstice

General Smudges

Feminine Focus

Aroma: resinous – sweetly musky with spicy overtones
Ceremonial Use: purifications; Venus, Moon and women's ceremonies
Significant Days: goddess and divine feminine days
Lunar Cycle: New and Full Moons; anytime, but especially 3rd and 4th
    quarter

Preparation Notes: Crush the cardamom pods, myrrh, sandalwood and valerian root, if necessary, and grind into a rough powder. Add thyme and blue vervain, and blend.

1/2 cup	cardamom pod	1 part
1 cup	myrrh resin	2 parts
1/2 cup	sandalwood	1 part
1/4 cup	thyme	1/2 part
1/2 cup C, 1/4 cup P	valerian root	1 part
1/2 cup	vervain, blue	1 part

The warm aroma and purifying qualities of the lunar myrrh and sandalwood are paired with the purification punch of solar blue vervain and thyme. Valerian provides relaxed feminine grounding, while cardamom adds spice and pays tribute to Venus, the goddess of love.

Lunar Purification

Aroma: resinous – sweetly musky
Ceremonial Use: purifications; women's, fertility, Moon and water
    ceremonies
Significant Days: goddess and divine feminine days; New and Full Moons;
Holi & Divali – Hindu; lunar Beltane, Lammas, Samhain & Imbolc – pagan,
Vesak & Bodhi Day – Buddhist; Passover, Rosh Hashana & Sukkot – Jewish

Lunar Cycle: New and Full Moons; anytime, but especially 3rd and 4th quarter

Preparation Notes: Crush the calamus, myrrh and sandalwood, if necessary, then grind with the buchu into a rough powder. Add mugwort and wild lettuce and blend.

1/2 cup	buchu	1 part
1/2 cup C, 1/4 cup P	calamus root - optional	1 part
1 cup	mugwort	2 parts
1 cup	myrrh resin	2 parts
1 cup	sandalwood	2 parts
1/4 cup	wild lettuce root - optional	1/2 part

This recipe produces a beautiful fluid smoke with a sweet, relaxing aroma. Mugwort, an herb of the Moon, is the core lunar connection. It imparts a bit of a buzz and aids in dream divination. Myrrh and sandalwood provide the base aroma and purifying strength.

The optional calamus and wild lettuce roots contribute spicy notes and are slightly trance inducing, but should not be used with children, teens or anyone on medication for psychiatric conditions. Pregnant and nursing women should avoid mugwort.

Masculine Manna

Aroma: spicy – with a touch of sweet
Ceremonial Use: purifications; Mars and Sun ceremonies; warrior and men's ceremonies
Significant Days: equinoxes and seasonal dates; god and divine masculine days
Lunar Cycle: New and Full Moons; anytime, but especially 3rd and 4th quarter

Preparation Notes: Crush the allspice, cinnamon, clove, copal, dandelion root and frankincense, if necessary, and then grind into a rough powder. Add hyssop and wood and wood betony and blend. Dust with benzoin resin and blend again.

1/4 cup	allspice	1 part
2 tbsp	benzoin resin	1/2 part
1/4 cup	cinnamon bark	1 part
2 tbsp	clove bud	1/2 part
1/4 cup	copal	1 part
1/4 cup C, 2 tbsp P	dandelion root	1 part
1/2 cup	frankincense	2 parts
1/4 cup	hyssop	1 part
1/4 cup	wood betony	1 part

This is a spicy smudge with fire and vigor that produces a dense, intense smoke. It energizes while being very grounding, yet packs a purification punch.

Solar (Sage) Purification

Aroma: herbaceous – sharp and resinous
Ceremonial Use: purifications; Sun and fire ceremonies; god and divine masculine days
Significant Days: Summer Solstice
Lunar Cycle: New Moon; anytime, but especially 3rd and 4th quarter

Preparation Notes: Break up or grind the bay laurel into medium-sized pieces. Add rosemary, white sage and yerba santa and grind to a rough powder. Blend in hyssop, sprinkle with juniper oil and blend again. Yerba santa has a strong musty smell, so increase the cedar, juniper or rosemary if you prefer.

1/2 cup	bay laurel	1 part
1/4 cup	cedar tips	1/2 part
1/4 cup	hyssop	1/2 part
15 to 20 drops	juniper oil	15 to 20 drops
1 cup	rosemary	2 parts
2 cups	sage, white	4 parts
1 cup	yerba santa	2 parts

My first and still most popular smudge. A strong sage smudge can strip your aura clean, leaving the person smudged without protection. In this blend, after hyssop pushes out the negativity and sage takes it away yerba santa provides a protective wrap. Bay laurel, cedar, rosemary and juniper provide additional purification and protection, while adding a green sharpness to the aroma. Be sure to use the Salvia apina sold by herb outlets, and not the "sage" found growing wild in the Southwest, which is often an artemisia with far different qualities.

Seasonal Smudges

Spring Equinox

Aroma: floral – with a bit of lemon and mint

Preparation Notes: Crush the copal resin and vetivert root, if necessary. Blend with remaining ingredients.

2 tbsp	acacia (gum Arabic)	1/2 part
2 tbsp	benzoin resin	1/2 part
1/2 cup	copal resin	2 parts
1/4 cup	elder flower	1 part
1/2 cup	hops	2 parts
1/2 cup	lavender	2 parts
1/2 cup	lemon balm	2 parts
1/4 cup	passionflower	1 part
1/4 cup	pennyroyal	1 part
1/2 cup	rose buds	2 parts
1/4 cup	sweet woodruff	1 part
1 cup C, 1/2 cup P or 15 to 20 drops	vetivert root or essential oil	2 parts or 15 to 20 drops

Spring florals with lemon and mint herbs are evocative of a soft spring breeze. Uplifts the mood and brightens the mind, always makes people smile. Use after an intense ceremony to take the edge off. Also works for summer rituals.

Beltane or Midsummer Bonfire

Aroma: herbaceous – slightly sharp and resinous

Preparation Notes: Blend together.

1/2 cup	elder flower	1 part
1/4 cup	frankincense	1/2 part
1 cup	rosemary	2 parts
1 cup	slippery elm bark	2 parts
1/2 cup	St. John's wort	1 part
1/4 cup	sweet woodruff	1/2 part
1/2 cup	vervain, blue	1 part
1/2 cup	wood betony	1 part

Rather than a risky running leap through a Beltane or Summer Solstice bonfire, pass through smoke infused with herbs that facilitate the holidays' qualities. Rosemary salutes the Sun and provides the bulk of the aroma, with blue vervain adding to the purifying power. Slippery elm and wood betony repair quarrels, carrying on the "burying the hatchet" part of Beltane rituals. St. John's wort brings in the solar focus and adds the love divination so important to Summer Solstice. Sweet woodruff also deepens the solar emphasis and softens the aroma.

Summer Solstice

Aroma: resinous – with vanilla, spice and a touch of sharpness

Preparation Notes: Crush the angelica root, cinnamon, and acacia, and benzoin, copal and frankincense resins, if necessary, and grind into a rough powder. Add remaining ingredients and blend.

2 tbsp	acacia (gum Arabic)	1/4 part
1/4 cup C, 2 tbsp P	angelica root	1/2 part
2 tbsp	benzoin resin	1/4 part
1/2 cup	cedar tips	1 part
1/2 cup	chamomile	1 part
1/2 cup	cinnamon bark chips	1 part
1/2 cup	copal resin	1 part
1 cup	frankincense resin	2 parts
1 cup	mullein	2 parts
1/4 cup	St. John's wort	1/2 part
1/4 cup	vervain, blue	1/2 part

A mélange of powerful tree resins and solar herbs. A spirit-arousing blend perfect for invoking the Sun, it has a challenging, complex aroma that stimulates the mind and imagination. Useful in ceremonies on other seasonal dates and tributes to solar deities.

Autumn Equinox

Aroma: spicy – with a touch of sweet

Preparation Notes: Crush the allspice, cinnamon, clove, copal, dandelion root and frankincense, if necessary, and then grind into a rough powder. Add benzoin resin, hyssop and wood betony and blend.

1/4 cup	allspice	1 part
2 tbsp	benzoin resin	1/2 part
1/4 cup	cardamom seed	1 part
1/4 cup	cinnamon bark chips	1 part
1/4 cup	clove bud	1/2 part
1/2 cup	copal resin	2 parts
1/4 cup	dandelion root	1 part
1/2 cup	frankincense resin	2 parts
1/4 cup	hyssop	1 part
1/2 cup	mugwort	2 parts

Spices and tree resins bring to mind warm bonfires and the forests of fall. A pleasant blend to pay tribute to the bounty of the planet, so applicable for fertility ceremonies.

Winter Solstice

Aroma: resinous – with herbs, evergreen and balsam

Preparation Notes: Crumble the bay laurel. Crush the angelica and licorice root, and copal and myrrh resin, if needed. Grind with bay laurel, poplar buds and white sage into a rough powder. Add sacred basil, juniper berry and rosemary and blend. Sprinkle with cypress oil and blend again.

1/4 cup	angelica root	1/2 part
1/4 cup	basil, sacred	1/2 part
1/4 cup	bay laurel	1/2 part
1/4 cup	cedar tips	1/2 part
1/2 cup	copal resin	1 part
10 to 20 drops	cypress essential oil	10 to 20 drops
1/4 cup C, 2 tbsp P	licorice root	1/2 part
1/2 cup	juniper berry	1 part
1/4 cup	myrrh resin	1/2 part
1/2 cup	poplar buds (Balm of Gilead)	1 part
1 cup	rosemary	2 parts
1/2 cup	sage, white	1 part

Evergreens and tree resins, plus the bold aromas of sacred basil, rosemary and sage, evoke a winter fireplace. Also superb for using at Imbolc and Candlemas, and in mid-winter New Year's observances including Tet (Southeast Asia) and Losar (Tibetan).

Specialized Smudges

These smudges are very unique. All are meant to be inhaled which produces a mildly altered mental state useful for meditation and trance. To preserve your lung health, always include the Lung Buffer blend. The active ingredients can also be absorbed through the skin if the smudge is done skyclad, or in the nude.

The cautions: Stand far enough back so that the smoke you inhale is cool. Do not inhale warm or hot smoke. Mind-altering blends are to be used only by adults in a private setting. Partake gradually and at a slow pace so that you can judge your dose. These blends are not for use by children or teens. They are not appropriate for anyone on psychiatric medication or for pregnant or nursing women. Do not drive or operate machinery on these blends.

Lung Buffer

Aroma: herbaceous – warm and spicy

Preparation Notes: Crush the pleurisy root, if necessary, and grind finely. Add the remaining herbs, which will be fluffy and somewhat difficult to mix.

1/2 cup	coltsfoot	1 part
1/2 cup	horehound and/or great mullein	1 part
1/4 cup	lungwort	1/2 part
1/8 cup C, 1/2 cup P	pleurisy root	1/4 part

This recipe is based on moist herbs high in mucilage that are known to sooth the lungs when inhaled as smoke. Coltsfoot has an extremely attractive aroma and is integral to non-tobacco smoking blends.

Deep Meditation

Aroma: herbaceous – sweet musk
Ceremonial Use: spiritual communions; trances; meditation
Significant Days: Full Moons; Wesak

Preparation Notes: Crush the mandrake root and myrrh, if necessary, and grind into a rough powder. Add anise seed, mugwort, scullcap (skullcap), blue vervain and wild lettuce, plus Lung Buffer, and blend.

2 tbsp	anise seed	1/4 part
2 tbsp C, 1 tbsp P	mandrake root	1/4 part
1/2 cup	mugwort	1 part
1/4 cup	myrrh resin	1/2 part
1/2 cup	scullcap	1 part
2 tbsp	vervain, blue	1/4 part
1/2 cup	wild lettuce root	1 part
1/4 cup	Lung Buffer Blend	1/2 part

This blend can induce deep alpha and theta states, and assists with vivid dreaming. The scullcap makes it very soothing to the nerves. Myrrh and mugwort open the emotions to the mind-expanding effects of wild lettuce and mandrake. Use this blend sparingly.

Divination & Dream Enhance

Aroma: herbaceous – sweet musk and spice
Ceremonial Use: dream divination
Significant Days: Full Moons; Summer Solstice

Preparation Notes: Crush the galangal root, if necessary, then grind with the buchu into a rough powder. Add St. John's wort, wild lettuce and wood betony, plus Lung Buffer, and blend.

1/4 cup	buchu	1/2 part
1/2 cup C, 1/4 cup P	galangal root	1 part
1/2 cup	mugwort	1 part
1/4 cup	St. John's wort	1/2 part
1/4 cup	wild lettuce root	1/2 part
1/2 cup	wood betony	1 part
1/4 cup	Lung Buffer	1/2 part

This blend helps us enter deep alpha and theta states with herbs that inspire vivid and sometimes prophetic dreaming. Use this blend sparingly.

Libido Lift

Aroma: herbaceous – warm and spicy
Ceremonial Use: women's and fertility ceremonies
Significant Days: Beltane

Preparation Notes: Crush the cardamom pods, coriander seed, mandrake root, muira pauma and vetivert root, if necessary, and grind into a rough powder. Be sure the mandrake and muira pauma are ground up well. Add anise seed, damiana, patchouli, yerba mate and Lung Buffer and blend. Sprinkle with clary sage oil and blend again.

2 tbsp	anise seed	1/4 part
1/2 cup	cardamom pod	1 part
1/4 cup	coriander seed	1/2 part
1 cup	damiana	2 parts
1 tbsp C, 1 1/2 cup P	mandrake root	1/8 part
1/2 cup C, 1/4 cup P	muira pauma	1 part

I/2 cup	patchouli	I part
15 to 20 drops	sage, clary oil	15 to 20 drops
I cup C, I/2 cup P or 15 to 20 drops	vetivert root or essential oil	2 parts or 15 to 20 drops
I/2 cup	yerba mate	I part
I/4 cup	Lung Buffer	I/2 part

This is a blend of aphrodisiac herbs with an emphasis on the female libido. The spicy cardamom and musky patchouli make a luscious aroma base that supports the leafy spiciness of damiana and yerba mate. The deep aroma masks the harsh but effective muira pauma and mandrake. Be careful with this blend, it really is potent.

Trance

Aroma: earthy – peppery ginger with musky undertones
Ceremonial Use: spiritual communion; trances; drumming
Significant Days: Full Moons

Preparation Notes: Crush the angelica, calamus, dandelion and galangal roots and kava kava, if necessary, into a rough powder. Add anise, damiana, mugwort and Lung Buffer, and blend. Sprinkle with clary sage oil and blend again.

I cup C, I/2 cup P	angelica root	2 parts
2 tbsp	anise seed	I/4 part
I/2 cup C, I/4 cup P	calamus root	I part
I/2 cup	damiana	I part
I/2 cup C, I/4 cup P	dandelion root	I part
I cup C, I/2 cup P	galangal root	2 parts
I cup C, I/2 cup P	kava kava	2 parts
I cup C, I/2 cup P	mugwort	2 parts
I cup C, I/2 cup P	myrrh	2 parts
15 to 20 drops	sage, clary oil	15 to 20 drops
I cup	Lung Buffer	2 parts

Here we have the hit parade of psychotropic roots, plus some trippy leaves and woods. Burn these herbs on large amounts of very hot charcoal. They are all somewhat psychedelic, hallucinatory and visionary with a lustful edge. The smoke can be somewhat harsh; if so, increase the Lung Buffer.

Smoke as Divine Conduit
From Your Hand to the Divine

With intent, the herbs or incense are lit, transforming into smoke that curls and swirls to the sky, bearing a message that is longing for receipt. Perhaps presented as an honoring, an acknowledgement, a sign of respect. Or as an offering, given from the heart without expectation of return, though hopes for one. Possibly a sacrifice, something relinquished for the sake of another. In each case, smoke provides a bridge between sacred and mundane realms.

Smoke prayers, for prayers in almost every culture go up. In Tibetan temple rituals, the aromas might include juniper, rhododendron, tamarisk, margosa and pine. Hindu temples are redolent with nag champa incense and the unique sweet of the Ailanthus malabarica tree's resin called halmaddi. Buddhist sanctuaries bloom with every aroma imaginable, all supported by the gentle round smell of sandalwood. Shinto temples are grounded in the dense aroma of agar wood.

In the west, the familiar waft of frankincense and myrrh follow the path of Psalm 141, verse 2: "Let my prayer be directed as incense in thy sight." The intricate aroma of ketoret, with its additional calamus, cinnamon, galbanum, saffron and more, has blessed the high Jewish temples for millennia. For their smoke prayers, North American indigenous in the temperate regions turn to sage, sweetgrass and evergreens, with copal resin favored in the tropical south.

Burnt Offerings & Smoke Prayers

When ancient Jews made their most important prayers to the divine, these were accompanied by burnt offerings. The most valuable item to sacrifice back then was livestock. The usual method was to offer animal fat to a sacred fire while sharing the cooked flesh for food. Sensible in times of scarity, but seems more like a messy barbeque! Offering an entire animal, a deeply sacred act, was termed a holocaust, which is where the WW II tragedy got its name.

This book is dedicated to a more humane method of sacrificial giving through the use of plant material. The act of sacrifice is simply giving up something of value. Sacrificing sacred herbs adds to that the spiritual and psychological qualities associated with the plants used. Burning calamus root evokes the element of water and inhaling the smoke can open the subconscious, while frankincense is fiery and snaps the conscious into awareness.

Burning herbs for smudge is all about producing volumes of smoke, but burnt offerings or smoke prayers are more focused on the aroma, which can impart a powerful effect on the mind and heart, serving as aromatherapy for groups. The aromas tend to be more sacred than traditional burnt offerings, though some men liken the smell of barbeque to a religious experience.

Rather than the refined and distilled quality of incense, by burning the bulk source plant material a much more direct connection between plant power and spiritual intent is created. Just as the case with smudge sticks, plants suitable for incense are limited, while those for burnt offerings and smoke prayers are nearly limitless, allowing you to fine tune a burning blend for any holy day, ceremony or personal need.

Burnt offerings and smoke prayers are wonderfully suited for addressing emotional and psychological as well as spiritual issues, much as shamans do through their ceremonies. By utilizing aroma and the visceral sensations of fire and smoke, burning-based rituals can get around conscious blocks and break through to core truths.

Making a Smoke Prayer

Hold the loose herbs in your hand and infuse with intent. Sprinkle the herbs onto hot embers so that only smoke, not flames, is produced. Inhale strongly, but do not take the smoke into lungs (unless partaking of blends in the Psyche recipe section). Keeping your mouth slightly open will enhance the aromas. If you wish, allow the smoke to envelope the entire body as a smudge. More info can be found in the **Smoke-Based Ceremonies** section.

Some of these offering blends are capable of attracting serious spiritual energy. Keep a small, well-sealed container of fumitory or asafoetida on hand. On rare occasions, spiritual energy raised may not be friendly, causing attendees to get anxious or fearful. If you sense this may be the case, toss fumitory on embers to disperse malevolent energies, or in the case of super-stinky asafetida, disperse everything, including people and animals.

Going Deeper

Some of the blends in the Psyche section of the offerings recipes feature herbs that can induce mildly altered mental states if inhaled deeply into the lungs. If intending to inhale an offering, always add the Lung Buffer herb blend into the herbs. This is important.

The cautions: Mind-altering herbs are to be used only by adults in a private setting. Partake gradually and at a slow pace so that you can judge your dose. Stand far enough away from the source so that the smoke is cool enough to inhale. Do not inhale warm or hot smoke. These herbs are not for use by children or teens. They are not appropriate for anyone on psychiatric medication or for pregnant or nursing women. Do not drive or operate machinery on these herbs.

Grasp the Silver Smoke Cord to the Sky

Burning herbs in ceremonies can be a very potent experience. The smoke makes manifest the elements of fire and air, highlighting their turbulent and fluid power in a dramatic way. At the same time, spiritual energies are attracted and nourished by the aromatic and ethereal substance. Engaging the senses through the smell of aromas and the heat of fire, ritual and ceremony becomes embodied, powerful, intensely memorable and utterly transforming.

Smoke Prayers & Offerings Recipes

Prepare to open the doors of perception through smoke prayers and offerings!

For the complete scoop of how to work with herbs, including details on purchase and storage, please see the chapter **Herbal 101**. But the crib notes below will help you interpret the recipes.

Herb Basics

The recipes feature herbs as you would buy them from a store or web outlet. In general, ground up versions will lose their potency faster than larger and more intact pieces of herbs.

Essential oils	A few herbs such as clary sage are generally available only as an essential oil. But essential oils don't fare so well on the high heat of charcoal.
Flowers	Flowers are sold as dried petals or complete blossoms.

Leaves	Leafy herbs are usually sold as dried leaves that have been cut into 1/2 inch or smaller pieces and sifted for stems. A few herbs like bay laurel are sold whole and then hand crushed.
Resins	Resins are usually sold in plastic-like masses ranging in size from small pearls to sizable chunks that are easy to crush. Some resins are sold as powders.
Roots	Roots are usually sold in small chunks of dried roots. They can be very hard! Unless you have a good sturdy grinder, buy roots powdered when possible.
Woods	Woods are usually sold as small chunks or shavings.

Here are a few abbreviations used in the recipes:
- Tbsp for Tablespoon
- Tsp for Teaspoon
- C for Chunks
- P for Powdered
- W for Whole

Using the Blends

Basic designations of significant Moons, seasonal dates, holy days and ceremonial situations are listed for each herbal blend. More ideas on how to use the blends are in the section **Smoke-Based Ceremonies**.

Smoke Prayers & Offerings Recipes

SPIRITUAL	Moon Commune
	Passages
	Spirit Food
	Sun Salutation
	Tree Temple

PSYCHE	Chill Out
	Grounding
	Love Attract
	Manifesting
	Mental Focus
	Mood Lifter
	Opening
	Releasing

ELEMENTAL	Air
	Earth
	Fire
	Water

Spiritual

Moon Commune

Aroma: resinous – sweetly musky and warm
Ceremonial Use: purifications; women's, fertility and water ceremonies
Significant Days: goddess and divine feminine days; New and Full Moons;
    Holi and Divali – Hindu; lunar Beltane, Lammas, Samhain and
    Imbolc – pagan; Vesak and Bodhi Day – Buddhist; Passover, Rosh
    Hashana and Sukkot - Jewish

Preparation Notes: Crush the myrrh and sandalwood, if necessary, and then grind with the buchu into a rough powder. Add mugwort and wild lettuce, if desired, and blend.

1/4 cup	buchu - optional	1/2 part
1/2 cup	mugwort	1 part
1 cup	myrrh resin	2 parts
1 cup	sandalwood	2 parts
1/2 cup	wild lettuce root - optional	1 part

Burn these lunar herbs as an offering to the Moon. Based on mugwort, herb of the Moon, myrrh and sandalwood, it is a deeply psychic and emotional blend. If children, teens or anyone on medication for psychiatric illness are not present, you can deepen the impact by including buchu and wild lettuce to expand the mind. Pregnant and nursing women should avoid mugwort.

Passages

Aroma: resinous – with much spice and sharpness
Ceremonial Use: cremations; funerals and memorial services
Significant Days: Day of the Dead; Divali - Hindu; Obon – Shinto;
  Samhain - pagan

Preparation Notes: Crush the copal, elder wood, mandrake root, myrrh, poplar bud and sandalwood, if necessary, and then grind into a rough and very sticky powder. Add anise seed, basil, Dittany of Crete and rosemary and blend. Sprinkle with cypress oil and blend again.

2 tbsp	anise seed	1/2 part
1/4 cup	basil	1 part
1 cup	copal resin	4 parts
10 to 20 drops	cypress oil	10 to 20 drops
1/4 cup	Dittany of Crete	1 part
1/4 cup	elder wood	1 part
2 tbsp	mandrake root	1/2 part
1 cup	myrrh resin	4 parts
1/2 cup	poplar bud (Balm of Gilead)	2 parts
1/4 cup	rosemary	1 part
1/2 cup	sandalwood	2 parts

For use at the end of life, this recipe features herbs that honor the deceased and assist their passages, either from the physical body or between worlds. Use this blend to dress the body before burial or cremation, or to toss into the grave. Burn the blend at memorial services, funerals and ancestor observances.

Spirit Food

Aroma: resinous – sweet with a slight sharp note
Ceremonial Use: ancestor remembrances; funerals and memorial services;
  evocations and honorings of spirits and spirit guides
Significant Days: Day of the Dead; Samhain – pagan; Divali - Hindu

Preparation Notes: Crush the copal, myrrh and poplar bud, if necessary, and grind into a rough and very sticky powder. Add Dittany of Crete and benzoin and blend.

1/8 cup	benzoin	1/4 part
1 cup	copal resin	2 parts
1/4 cup	Dittany of Crete	1/2 part
1/4 cup	myrrh resin	1/2 part
1/2 cup	poplar bud (Balm of Gilead)	1 part

Burn these herbs to nourish the spirit world. Copal is an integral part of Day of the Dead ceremonies in Mexico. Poplar buds (Balm of Gilead) assists in releasing the spirits from their domain and Dittany of Crete helps them to manifest in ours. Benzoin assists humans to astral project into theirs. The lush smoke beckons to spiritual entities and sustains a connection from beyond the veil.

Sun Salutation

Aroma: resinous – with vanilla, spice and a touch of sharpness
Ceremonial Use: men's ceremonies; Sun and fire ceremonies; god and divine masculine days
Significant Days: Solstices, Equinoxes

Preparation Notes: Crush the angelica root, cinnamon, copal and frankincense, if necessary, and grind into a rough powder. Add St. John's wort and blend. Lightly dust with acacia (gum Arabic) and benzoin and blend again.

2 tbsp	acacia (gum Arabic)	1/4 part
1/4 cup C, 2 tbsp P	angelica root	1/2 part
2 tbsp	benzoin resin	1/4 part
1/4 cup	chamomile	1/2 part
1/2 cup	cinnamon bark	1 part
1 cup	copal resin	2 parts
1 cup	frankincense resin	2 parts
1/2 cup	St. John's wort	1 part

A medley of solar herbs with high spiritual vibrations. Frankincense, the most fiery of all the resins, serves as the aromatic base, with copal adding a bit of mellow sweetness. Angelica and St. John's wort impart visionary and divination qualities, with acacia (gum Arabic) and benzoin contributing warm undertones. Cinnamon bark chips adds fire and spice.

Tree Temple

Aroma: resinous – sweetly sharp with vanilla and spice
Ceremonial Use: all sacred gatherings; World Tree ceremonies
Significant Days: Yule, Arbor Day

Preparation Notes: Crush the agarwood, copal, dhoop incense, dragon's blood, frankincense, myrrh and sandalwood, if necessary, and grind into a rough powder. Sprinkle the cypress oil on top and blend. Lightly dust with acacia (gum Arabic) and benzoin powders and blend.

2 tbsp	acacia (gum Arabic)	1/4 part
2 tbsp	benzoin resin	1/4 part
1/2 cup	copal resin	1 part
10 to 15 drops	cypress oil	10 to 15 drops
2 tbsp	dragon's blood resin	1/4 part
1/2 cup	frankincense resin	1 part
1/2 cup	myrrh resin	1 part
1/2 cup	sandalwood	1 part

Optional Additions

2 tbsp C, 1 1/2 tsp P	agar wood	1/4 part
2 tbsp	halmaddi resin via Nag Champa Incense, powdered or crushed cone	1/4 part
2 tbsp C, 1 1/2 tsp P	palo santo	1/4 part

This is a great all-around aromatic temple blend that enhances any sacred setting or occasion. It's a perfect medley of mind, spirit and emotion, Sun and Moon, and all four elements. Breathing this aroma is to take communion with the World Tree and merge with our history as human beings. Sharp frankincense and sweet myrrh are sacred resins from the desert Middle East. Copal is the primary sacred resin of Mexico and South America. Dragon's blood resin is held sacred by pagans and Wiccans. Acacia is an ancient tree with a sacred past. Benzoin is a tree resin that lifts the mind and binds aromas together.

Optional Additions: These ingredients are more expensive and difficult to find, generally sold only in online specialty stores. All are scarce. Be sure to buy only sustainably harvested or farm and plantation raised versions. Agar wood, favored by followers of Shinto, Hindu and even Islam, is extremely expensive compared to the other ingredients. Nag champa incense is included as a source of the sacred halmaddi resin from the Ailanthus malabarica tree of India. Palo santo (Burseara graveolens) is sacred to the indigenous people of the Andes.

Psyche

Some of these blends are suitable for inhaling or skyckad (nude) smudging. Please observe these cautions: Stand far enough back so that the smoke you inhale is cool. Do not inhale warm or hot smoke. Mind-altering blends are to be used only by adults in a private setting. Partake gradually and at a slow pace so that you can judge your dose. These blends are not for use by children or teens. They are not appropriate for anyone on psychiatric medication or for pregnant or nursing women. Do not drive or operate machinery on these blends.

Chill Out

Aroma: resinous – warm and musky
Ceremonial Use: to relax the body and reduce anxiety

Preparation Notes: Crush the myrrh and valerian root, if necessary, and grind into a rough powder. Blend with mugwort.

1/2 cup	mugwort	1 part
1/2 cup	myrrh resin	1 part
1/2 cup	valerian root	1 part
1/4 cup	Lung Buffer	1/2 part

Very useful for calming overly aroused or agitated people, or to help a festival crowd wind down and get ready for sleep. Inhalable and suitable for nude smudging; please read the cautions detailed at the beginning of this section. Pregnant and nursing women should avoid mugwort.

Grounding

Aroma: earthy – with a sharp edge
Ceremonial Use: to center and aid with focus

Preparation Notes: Crush the vetivert root, if necessary, and grind into a rough powder. Blend with patchouli and blue vervain. Sprinkle with cypress oil and blend again.

5 to 10 drops	cypress oil	5 to 10 drops
I cup	patchouli	2 parts
1/4 cup C, 2 tbsp P or 5 to 10 drops	vetivert root or essential oil	1/2 part or 5 to 10 drops
1/2 cup	vervain, blue	I part

Patchouli grounds by awakening the lower three chakras, while the very earthy aroma of vetivert is centering to the extreme. Blue vervain is goddess-strong in its Earth manifestation and cypress is that rare resin-laden tree with an Earth element designation, lending a great power plus mind-awakening boost. A great offering to prepare participants for rituals and to assist individuals who feel scattered. Use it to quiet down a feisty crowd before ceremonies.

Love Attracting

Aroma: herbaceous – warm and spicy
Ceremonial Use: love and fertility ceremonies

Preparation Notes: Crush the cardamom pods, coriander seed, mandrake root, muira pauma and vetivert root, if necessary, and grind into a rough powder. Be sure the mandrake and muira pauma are ground up well. Add anise seed, damiana, patchouli, yerba mate and Lung Buffer and blend. Sprinkle with clary sage oil and blend again.

1/2 cup	cardamom pod	I part
1/4 cup	coriander seed	1/2 part
I cup	damiana	2 parts
I tbsp C. I ½ tsp P	mandrake root	1/8 part
1/2 cup	patchouli	I part
15 to 20 drops	sage, clary oil	15 to 20 drops
1/2 cup	slippery elm bark	2 parts
I cup C, 1/2 cup P or 15 to 20 drops	vetivert root or essential oil	2 parts or 15 to 20 drops
1/4 cup	wood betony	I part
1/2 cup	yerba mate	I part
1/4 cup	Lung Buffer	1/2 part

When you feel warm and attractive, partners are attracted to you. This is a blend of aphrodisiac herbs with an emphasis on the female libido. The spicy cardamon and musky patchouli make a luscious aroma base that supports the leafy spiciness of damiana and yerba mate. Inhalable and suitable for nude smudging; please read the cautions detailed at the beginning of this section.

Manifesting

Aroma: resinous – spicy and bright with a bit of warm undertones
Ceremonial Use: New Moon services; setting intentions

Preparation Notes: Crush the copal and dandelion root, if necessary, and grind into a rough powder. Blend in the clove, cardamom seed, cinnamon bark chips, clove bud and coriander. Dust with benzoin and blend again.

1/4 cup	allspice	5 to 10 drops
1/4 cup C, 2 tbsp P	angelica root	2 parts
2 tbsp	benzoin resin	5 to 10 drops
1/4 cup	cardamom seed	1 part
1/4 cup	cinnamon bark chips	1 part
1/4 cup	clove bud	1 part
1/2 cup	copal resin	1 part
1/4 cup	coriander	1 part
1/4 cup C, 2 tbsp P	dandelion root	1 part

As a metaphor of concentrated effort and future planning, seeds hold intent well, as do roots with their symbolism of grounding for longevity. The spices of this blend – allspice, cardamom, cinnamon, clove and coriander – are all associated with prosperity. Dandelion root is a strong and nurturing root, while angelica accesses spiritual realms. Copal helps the seedy blend burn and brightens the mind to hold the intent.

Mental Focus

Aroma: herbaceous – with a resinous edge
Ceremonial Use: to sharpen focus or sober up

Preparation Notes: Crush the frankincense, if necessary, and grind into a rough powder. Lightly grind the bay laurel and rosemary and blend with frankincense. Dust with benzoin and blend. Sprinkle with camphor oil and blend again.

1/2 cup	bay laurel	1 part
2 tbsp	benzoin resin	1/4 part
15 to 20 drops	camphor oil	15 to 20 drops
1/2 cup	frankincense resin	1 part
1/2 cup	rosemary	1 part

Burn this blend to bring about a clarity that's helpful when an alert mind is needed. Great for those times at festivals when people have had too much fun with intoxicants and sexual proclivities. It also aids in waking up sleepy people or keeping them awake.

Mood Lifter

Aroma: herbaceous – with floral and citrus notes
Ceremonial Use: to instill a happy vibe, counter depression and anxiety

Preparation Notes: Crush copal, if necessary, and grind into a rough powder. Mix with remaining herbs. Sprinkle with oils and blend again.

1/4 cup	bergamot oil	1 part
1/4 cup	clary sage oil	1 part
1/4 cup	copal resin	1 part
1/2 cup	lavender	2 parts
1/4 cup	lemon balm	2 parts
1/4 cup	rosemary	1 part

Depressed about your life? Tired after a long winter or hard summer? This offering will lift your spirits. Use in rituals to let go of grief, sadness or depression. Effective as a sadness-be-gone smudge. Excellent blend to create a bright atmosphere at social gatherings. Perfect at weddings.

Opening

Aroma: earthy – with hints of sharp and spice
Ceremonial Use: to open the heart and emotions

Preparation Notes: Crush the myrrh and valerian root, if necessary, and grind into a rough powder. Add remaining herbs and blend.

1/4 cup	calamus root	I part
1/4 cup	cardamom pod	I part
1/2 cup	coltsfoot	2 parts
1/2 cup	myrrh resin	2 parts
1/4 cup	poplar bud (Balm of Gilead)	I part
1/4 cup	valerian root	I part
1/4 cup	Lung Buffer	1/2 part

Valerian root relaxes deeply, myrrh resin releases the emotions, poplar bud liberates the psyche and calamus root evokes a mild trance state. These all work together at opening the subconscious up to new patterns. Cardamom and coltsfoot impart a pleasant mood. Inhalable and suitable for nude smudging; please read the cautions detailed at the beginning of this section.

Releasing

Aroma: resinous – spicy and musky with a hint of sweetness
Ceremonial Use: burning bowl services; habit breaking; separations and divorces

Preparation Notes: Crush the clove, coriander, galangal root, myrrh and slippery elm if necessary, and grind into a rough powder. Add hyssop, rosemary and wood betony and blend. Dust with benzoin and blend again.

2 tbsp	benzoin resin	1/2 part
1/4 cup	clove bud	I part
1/4 cup	coriander	I part
1/4 cup	galangal root	I part
1/4 cup	hyssop	I part
1/2 cup	myrrh resin	2 parts
1/4 cup	rosemary	I part
1/2 cup	slippery elm bark	2 parts
1/4 cup	wood betony	I part

It can be hard to let go. Burning this herbal blend gives focus to our intentions for change. Burn these herbs with slips of paper listing who or what is to be released. This blend facilitates the separation of unhealthy relationships and helps end gossip and malingering. It's also helpful for breaking any kind of pattern. I have had some howling good ceremonies around the hibachi with this one as women shouted out their released burdens and danced. This blend works well as a smudge.

Elemental

Air

Aroma: spicy – with warm undertones
Ceremonial Use: evoking the power of air and its attributes: intellect,
    ideas, invention
Significant Days: New and Full Moons in air signs, air deity days

Preparation Notes: Lightly grind hops, blend with anise and caraway. Dust with acacia (gum Arabic) and benzoin, and blend again.

1/4 cup	anise seed	1/2 part
2 tbsp	acacia (gum Arabic)	1/4 part
2 tbsp	benzoin resin	1/4 part
1/4 cup	caraway seed	1/2 part
1/2 cup	hops	1 part

Earth

Aroma: earthy – with a sharp edge
Ceremonial Use: evoking the power of earth and its attributes: stability,
    sustenance, wisdom
Significant Days: New and Full Moons in earth signs, earth deity days

Preparation Notes: Crush the vetivert root, if necessary, and grind into a rough powder. Blend with patchouli and blue vervain. Sprinkle with cypress oil and blend again.

5 to 10 drops	cypress oil	5 to 10 drops
1 cup	patchouli	2 parts
1/4 cup C, 2 tbsp P or 5 to 10 drops	vetivert root or essential oil	1/2 part or 5 to 10 drops
1/2 cup	vervain, blue	1 part

Fire

> Aroma: spicy – with a highlights of sharp and sweet
> Ceremonial Use: evoking the power of fire and its attributes: spirit, passion, creativity
> Significant Days: Summer and Winter Solstices, New and Full Moons in fire signs, fire deity days

Preparation Notes: Crush the allspice, angelica root, coriander, dragon's blood, frankincense and galangal root, if necessary, and grind into a rough powder. Add hyssop and blend.

1/4 cup	allspice	1 part
1/4 cup	angelica root	1 part
1/4 cup	coriander	1 part
1 tbsp	dragon's blood resin	1/4 part
1/4 cup	frankincense resin	1 part
1/4 cup	galangal root	1 part
1/4 cup	hyssop	1 part

Water

> Aroma: earthy – with hints of sharp and spice
> Ceremonial Use: evoking the power of water and its attributes: emotion, communication, subconscious
> Significant Days: New and Full Moons in water signs, water deity days

Preparation Notes: Crush the poplar bud, cardamom pod, myrrh, calamus root and valerian root, if necessary, and grind into a rough powder. Lightly grind the coltsfoot and blend with the other ingredients.

1/4 cup	calamus root	1 part
1/4 cup	cardamom pod	1 part
1/2 cup	coltsfoot	2 parts
1/2 cup	myrrh resin	2 parts
1/4 cup	poplar bud (Balm of Gilead)	1 part
1/4 cup	valerian root	1 part

Cauldron Circles
Smoke & Memories

Seasons turn, occasions arise, ceremonies come and go. How many do you remember and why?

Memorable ceremonies rely on vivid sensory sensations that take ritual beyond rote. Smoke-based ceremonies fully involve participants' five senses. The warmth, aroma and sensation of burning herbs provides enough distractions to occupy the conscious mind so that the subconscious is free to connect with the deep message being conveyed. Created are embodied moments that people can remember and call upon in their times of need.

I'd go bonkers if not for sacred smoke ceremonies a couple times a month. I light up the hibachi in my backyard at least every New Moon, sometimes by myself, sometimes with others, in what I call a Cauldron Circle. The neighbors have grown quite accustomed to the regular billows of aromatic smoke! I think they feel it keeps the mosquitoes down.

Brief suggestions for ceremonial uses and occasions, plus appropriate holy days, seasonal dates and lunar phases, are noted with each blend recipe. Here are some further ideas on full-fledged Caldron Circles using the herbal blends.

Circle Format

Everyone who leads ceremonies has their own unique approach. Below is an outline for a typical Cauldron Circle of mine. This chapter will explore each of these sections in depth.

- Circle Preparation
- Setting the Circle
- Smudge
- Smoke Prayers
- Finishing Smudge (optional)
- Concluding the Circle

Circle Preparation

My technique for creating a holy place outdoors is by strewing, a nice term for flinging dried herbs about. This lovely practice is covered in my book "Raw Herbs: Power Potpourris for Mood Enhancement & Strewing for Sacred Space."

If the energy of the site is not spiffy clean, clear the area first by strewing the whole area with the book's Positive Space herb mixture based on purifying herbs and negativity-absorbing carminative seeds. Define the space by strewing a protective boundary that contains the energy about to be raised and deflects intrusive forces. Use the Protection blend of herbs that projects a strong defensive feel.

Then gauge your circle participants' state of mind. If they're antsy from rushing around or battling traffic, shift them into a more agreeable mental frame by burning Mood Lifter with lavender and rosemary. If tension is evident, the aromatic mugwort and myrrh smoke of Chill Out will quickly remedy. If the participants project a distracted energy, center them with the earthy vetivert-based Grounding. Or if they're reticent, relax the resistance with Opening, a complex spice and resin blend that softens emotions.

See? Isn't this the coolest!

Setting the Circle

Kick off your Cauldron Circle with a burning of Spirit Food to nurture the Earth devas of where the gathering is held. You're visiting their realm; it's polite to offer a gift. Spirit Food's blend of resins, plus the poplar buds used to create Balm of Gilead, is attractive and nourishing to spiritual energies.

Rather than a formal calling of the elements, which tends to get rote, my Cauldron Circles usually accomplish that task with an elemental chant accompanied by hand motions. Here are a couple of traditional favorites:

> **Earth my body,**   *pat thighs*
> **Water my blood,**   *cradling/waving motion of arms*
> **Air my breath,**   *hands reaching out from mouth*
> **And fire my spirit.**   *clap hands in front of third eye*

> **The earth,**   *palms toward ground*
> **The air,**   *hands together and up the body center*
> **The fire,**   *clap in front of 3rd eye*
> **The water,**   *fingers in rain motions downward*
> **Return, return,**   *continue rain motion*
> **return, return.**

While the chant continues, burn the Tree Temple blend of sacred-tree resins that is balanced to include all four elements.

To go all out for a big-deal ceremony, station hibachis of hot embers at each of the directional points. Burn the corresponding elemental offering blends while calling the energies in.

Smudge

As preamble to the main Cauldron Circle smoke prayers ritual, a purifying smudge is the signal that shifts us from mundane to sacred.

The act of smudging can be conducted by a spiritual leader who sprinkles the herb blend on hot embers, creating a cloud of smoke that an individual or group can immerse themselves in. Or individual circle members can burn the herbs for their own private smudge. Make sure to become fully immersed in smoke. Lean over to smudge your chest and head, straddle the smoke to purify your private parts. Stick your rear, hands and feet in there, too – hokey-pokey it!

The strongly purifying Solar blend, featuring sage and yerba santa, goes well with seasonal start dates and other occasions determined by the Sun's placement. It'll banish even the most negative of auras. The gentler Lunar smudge, with its mugwort and myrrh, is perfect for New and Full Moons. It serves as a purification and blessing in one.

Seasonal smudges are great for equinoxes, solstices and mid-seasons, since their aromas evoke the specific times of year. A great way to bond with the seasonal energies, they're gentle and quite suitable for public gatherings with newbies. They also work well for offerings and smoke prayers. One exception is the Beltane & Midsummer blend that has a specific ritual covered later in this chapter.

The sweetly spicy Feminine Focus smudge blend was designed with initiation into women's mysteries in mind. It's also super for ceremonies in honor of specific goddesses or divine feminine figures, or those that acknowledge passage into the great female phases: maiden, mother, queen and crone. Masculine Manna is similarly suited for initiations and stage-of-life ceremonies, plus events honoring gods or divine masculine figures.

More details on working with smudges are in the chapter **Taking a Smoke Bath: Industrial-Strength Smudges for Tough Times**.

Smoke Prayers for Moons

The core of the Cauldron Circle is the smoke prayer ceremony, with participants performing their own personal rituals. The enigmatic imagery and vivid aromas create a dramatic ceremony that is extremely impactful. Simply hold the loose herbs in hand and infuse with intent. Then sprinkle the herbs to create smoke and allow the intentions to transform. Inhale the resulting aromas; keeping your mouth slightly open will enhance the effect.

New and Full Moons and seasonal celebrations tend to get big crowds – high church for the Earth-centered set.

For Full Moon events, the sight and smell of the silvery smoke tendrils of Moon Commune's soft myrrh and mugwort smoke reaching upward to the lunar orb is truly a magical experience. The blends Manifestation and Opening are also excellent for Moon ceremonies. Rituals for Full Moons tend to focus on bringing manifestations to positive conclusions, or opening up the mind and emotions to flowing lunar energy. It's also a great time to just go crazy – a little lunar release now and then is a good thing.

Holy days associated with Full Moons include:
- Holi, the Hindu holiday of spring and color, usually in March
- Passover, the Jewish holy day of faith usually in April
- Vesak, the celebration of Buddha's birth and enlightenment, usually in May
- Sukkot, the Jewish honoring of the Earth, usually in October

New Moon ceremonies are best done during the day, since the Moon is conjunct with the Sun on New Moons. Making a commitment to new attitudes, initiating a process, or beginning a project by burning herbs beneath the conjoined lunar and solar energies is empowering. Moon Commune is the go-to blend, but Manifestation also goes well with New Moons. Releasing is best in the 4th quarter prior to the new moon when it's easiest to let things go.

Holy days associated with New Moons include:
- Losar, the Tibetan New Year, usually in February
- Rosh Hashana, the Jewish New Year, usually in September
- Divali, the Hindu holiday of ancestors and light, usually in November

Every New and Full Moon falls in a specific astrological signs and each sign has an elemental designation. Use the Elemental offering blends to tap into the archetypal wisdom of the lunar astrological placements:

element	archetype	astro sign
Earth	Fertility	Taurus, Virgo and Capricorn
Air	Imagination	Gemini, Libra and Aquarius
Fire	Spirit	Aries, Leo and Sagittarius
Water	Emotion	Cancer, Scorpio and Pisces

Also see the cross-quarter seasonal Moons in the section below.

More details on working with smoke prayers are in the chapter **Smoke as Divine Conduit: From Your Hand to the Divine.**

Smoke Prayers for Seasons

Seasonal ceremonies also tend to be more resonant during the day owing to that visceral connection to the Sun that causes the seasons. This book features offering blends for Spring and Fall Equinoxes and Summer and Winter Solstices. The Sun Salutation blend is also effective for seasonal events. These rituals focus around what you want to manifest in the seasonal duration, or celebrate the metaphoric wisdom that each season offers.

A truly moving ritual for Yule or Winter Solstice is to burn Tree Temple. Inhaling this blend of resins from the world's sacred trees is like taking communion with the archetypal World Tree from which humankind first took sustenance and shelter. (Wassail and cake makes it even better!)

The seasonal midpoints, also called cross-quarters, fall roughly halfway between solstices and equinoxes. Though now observed on calendar dates, their original settings on New or Full Moons are far more powerful.

Cross Quarter	Season	Holiday	Date	Moon
Imbolc	Mid-Winter	Candlemas	Feb. 2	New Moon between Winter Solstice and Spring Equinox
Beltane	Mid-Spring	May Day	May 1	Full Moon between Spring Equinox and Summer Solstice
Lammas	Mid-Summer	Green Corn Harvest	Aug. 2	Full Moon between Summer Solstice and Autumn Equinox
Samhain	Mid-Autumn	Halloween, Day of the Dead	Oct. 31, Nov. 2	New Moon between Autumn Equinox and Winter Solstice

Traditional Beltane and Summer Solstice ceremonies often involve taking a running leap through a bonfire. Instead, bring greater meaning to these holy dates, and keep your short and curlies unsinged, with a naked immersion in smoke infused with herbs associated with the holidays. The Beltane & Midsummer blend features herbs that help facilitate the "burying the hatchet" part of Beltane rituals and herbs for love divination that is so entwined with Summer Solstice. This technique allows bonfire-style Beltane and Summer Solstice ceremonies to be held in urban settings.

Smoke Prayers for Personal Transformation

Perhaps my favorite ceremony is just a few close women friends in Cauldron Circle around the hot embers while working through intense issues. It's a shamanic approach to personal growth, using intentions along with smoke, sound and rhythm to remove emotional or psychological impediments that hinder spirituality, at the same time tapping into deep Earth energies. The dark of a nighttime setting emphasizes the intimacy.

My most requested smoke ceremony is Releasing, utilizing the transmutive power of smoke for letting go of blocks, situations and emotions that no longer serve. It features seeds that hold energetic intent plus herbs that promote transformation.

The complement to these includes Manifestation, also using the concentrated metaphor of seeds along with herbs that promote positive thinking. The blend Love Attract puts a romantic spin on that, with herbs that inspire heart connection along with a bit of physical lust for fun. The blend Opening emphasizes receptivity and being open emotionally.

Smoke rituals at outdoor funerals and memorial services can provide an essential cathartic experience. The blend Passages is rich with incense resins and sacred herbs associated with death. With heart felt sentiments relayed through burning herbs, the smoke reaching toward the heavens reminds the mourners of the eternal connection they will always share. The blend was originally developed to prepare bodies for cremation or burial.

Spirits and spirit guides can be invoked with the Spirit Food blend, so it pairs perfectly with seasonal ancestor remembrances like Day of the Dead, Divali, the Obon, and the Samhain.

More details on working with smoke prayers are in the chapter **Smoke as Divine Conduit: From Your Hand to the Divine**.

Finishing Smudge

Smoke prayers can venture into some intense emotional and psychological territory. A light smudge afterward can help lift any heaviness incurred. The floral Spring Equinox smudge is especially good for that, or use the Mood Lifter offering as a smudge.

Inhaling smoke can leave people light headed and intense transformation can make participants slightly disoriented. Before letting them loose, anchor them and their experiences further with Grounding. Or sharpen their mind with Mental Focus and sear that transformative work into deep memory. Both blends are offerings that can be used as smudges.

Concluding the Circle

The Tree Temple blend, with its mindful aroma, is an excellent conclusion to a Cauldron Circle, bringing participants back into real time. Because it is elementally balanced, burned with intent it can be used to release any elemental energies that were raised.

Trance Circles
Going Deep

Cauldron Circles tend to last an hour or two. Participants can achieve a spiritualized state, but they're all aware that afterwards they've got to drive, do errands and otherwise carry on with the basic tasks of living.

But in the right setting with ample time, a Trance Circle can take you deeper to amazing places. In these gatherings, special smudges are used to help participants achieve a mildly altered state that allows them to go deeper into the subconscious and spiritual realms.

Trance Circles are an active meditation done with spiritual intent, achieving a frame of mind that is physically alert yet deeply relaxed. They're perfect for drum circles, circle dances, moving meditations and chanting kirtans.

The herbal blends for Trance Circles are outlined in the Specialized sections of the smudge chapters. While they can be done clothed, it's best to be as naked as possible so that the herb's active ingredients get absorbed through the skin. These smudges can also be inhaled if desired.

Specialized smudges are best done in a private location with a small group that is already acquainted with each other. Set aside at least four hours for a Trance Circle. They're ideal for situations such as camping festivals where you don't have to drive home afterward

CHAPTER MENU	Circle Format
	Circle Prep, Elements & Smudge
	Smoke Prayers
	Specialized Smudges

Circle Format

Trance Circles are rather open-ended, allowing each participant to go as deep as they feel comfortable. But it's important to firmly establish a sacred frame of mind and set spiritual intent at the start so that the Trance Circle does not devolve into party. A typical one might go like this:

- Circle Preparation
- Setting the Circle
- Purification Smudge
- Smoke Prayers & Offerings
- Trance Smudge

Circle Prep, Elements & Smudge

Everything for circle site preparation outlined in **Cauldron Circles: Smoke & Memories** applies for Trance Circles. Strew the Positive Space herb blend to purify the space. Use an extra thick and wide perimeter strewing of Protection to define the circle area and support participants in relaxing deeply into their trance state.

Setting the circle is also the same as in Cauldron Circles with an offering of the Spirit Food blend. Lay it on thick for a Trance Circle! This blend both attracts spiritual energies to be present in our realm and facilitates our astral projection into theirs.

Trance Circles scan be initiated superbly with an extended session of shamanic drumming that emphasizes the upcoming wordless trance state. Burn the Tree Temple blend to honor the elements and sharpen participants' focus.

Acknowledge the sacredness of the trance state with a purification smudge. While all the General and Seasonal blends will work fine, the Lunar blend with its mildly psychic mugwort is an especially good preamble.

Smoke Prayers & Offerings

Here are some ideas for using recipes from the Psyche section of **Smoke Prayers & Offerings** to set your intent for the trance.

Do you want to tap into deep earth energies, perhaps to fuel an extended drumming session? Grounding is the blend for that. Need to remove blocks or let go of issues before entering a trance? No better blend than Releasing. Aiming for intuitive insight and psychic inspiration, or even communication with other realms? Opening is your blend. Have a purpose for your chant that is specific? Go with Manifestation.

Here are some ideas for using recipes from the Spiritual section of **Smoke Prayers & Offerings** to set your intent for the trance.

Doing your trance beneath the Full Moon? Then Moon Commune is a must for connecting with intuitive lunar energies. Trancing out in honor of a seasonal change or mid-point? Sun Salutation is your blend. Just want to set a spiritual mood? Tree Temple is perfect for that.

Specialized Smudges

Now we get to the core of the Trance Circle – the specialized skyclad smudges that are inhalable.

Be sure to read and follow all the instructions and cautions in the chapter **Taking a Smoke Bath: Industrial-Strength Smudges for Tough Times**, as well as those with each smudge recipe. These smudges are not suitable for anyone under 18, or who is pregnant, nursing or on psychiatric medication.

The main blend is Trance, based on psychotropic roots from around the world with additional mystic herbs. The powerhouse is galangal root from Southeast Asia. No only is it mildly psychedelic, a potent dose is useful in separating from old patterns, making breakthroughs during trance more likely. Angelica, medieval Europe's most popular trippy root, is visually stimulating, as is anise seed and damiana leaf. Calamus root, also known as sweet flag or sweet sedge, is contemplative yet peppy. Also slightly stimulating, yet hypnotic, is the wood of kava kava, the "mystic pepper" of the Pacific islands.

Libido Lifter, named for its frisky effect on women, opens the second chakra's creative center, unleashing imagination as well as sexual expression. Damiana, an aphrodisiac herb from Mexico, does the heavy lifting in this blend, aided by its male counterpart, tropical muira pauma wood. The rich earthiness of patchouli and vetivert keeps things grounded by enlivening the root chakra, and provides a warm base for anise, cardamom and coriander, all spices associated with congenial relationships.

If your trance needs are more contemplative, Deep Meditation is an excellent blend to accompany spirit journeys, shadow work and archetypal explorations. It's based on wild lettuce, which contains a mild opium-like substance that guides you into a deep theta brainwave state, aided by skullcap, an herbal nervine.

Continue the benefits of your trance by finishing with Dream Divination before you depart to bed. It features herbs associated with dreams that are deep, vivid and sometimes prophetic.

Utilize blends from the Psyche section of **Smoke Prayers & Offerings** to manage the trance state. Burn some Mental Focus if participants are too deeply entranced, or Mood Lifter if the trance process causes emotional distress. A round of Relaxation can be quite helpful to conclude the trance process.

Herbal 101
What You Need To Know To Work With Herbs

Working with ceremonial herbs for smudges and smoke prayers is like cooking or chemistry. Simple elemental building blocks are combined and catalyzed into something well beyond the individual parts.

Types of Ceremonial Herbs

The word "herb" may bring to mind the little flecks of green in your marinara or salsa. But herbs go well beyond leaves. Ceremonial herbs include flowers (so friendly), seeds, berries and buds (potently concentrated), bark and wood (rough and primeval), roots (mysterious and uber-powerful), and resins and saps (fantastic evocative aromas).

Bark & Wood
Most wood has a diffuse but solid energy that carries the metaphorical qualities of the trunk of a tree: bringing the light of Sun and the dark of Earth into a core of strength. Inner or outer layers of bark are used and come in a wide variety of textures. It takes a high heat to ignite wood and bark. The smoke, except for sandalwood and a few others, tends to be harsh, though the aroma of the plant carries forward nicely. Wood is usually sold as shreds or shavings.

Leaves

The herbiest parts of herbs are the leaves, those engines of photosynthesis and the great pranic breath of the planet. The aroma of burning leaves is often quite different from what they smell like fresh or dried. Use the lowest heat possible to burn leaves. They are most often sold as small cut pieces of dried leaves that are sifted for stems and seeds.

Resins & Saps

Resins are the most elite of ceremonial herbs and the priciest as well. Sap is a fluid that moves through trees, sort of like maple syrup in maple trees. In some trees, like frankincense, the extracted sap dries into heavy, dense pearls of resin for burning as incense. In others it dries into a powder. Similar methods are used to create a gum extract. When derived from sacred woods, these represent the blood of the tree. Inhaling the burning fragrance is to be in communion with the World Tree from which humankind developed.

But do remember that resins are heavy with natural hydrocarbons. (After all, turpentine is made from pine sap.) Resins will flame up when tossed on embers. Toss on too many and you'll find yourself with a rowdy fire. I once packed a Yule Log with resins that sent horizontal flames shooting out two feet when the log was lit during the ceremony. The hem of my long dress caught on fire in front of 200 folks who were both horrified and highly entertained by the little pyro-dance I did to put it out.

Roots

I love roots, so earthy, raw and resplendent with dark power. Larger tuberous roots, when fresh, can even be a pleasant chew. But the dried tuber pieces, usually the size of peas, are tough and very hard to grind. You have to pound on them quite a bit first. Consider buying them already powdered.

Seeds, Berries & Buds

These fertile capsules hold a concentrated energy and represent poised potential. As seeds burn they produce neat aroma bursts.

Buying Herbs

Bulk herbs can be found at many natural food stores, though the focus in grocery stores is usually on edible ones. Some alternative, counterculture and garden shops also carry them. To find a full array of herbs, metaphysical stores, especially those with a pagan bent, are your best bet. Some herbs like cardamom and star anise are best bought at Asian ethnic stores. But unless you're in a big city or uber hip area, retail herbal pickings can be slim.

But the more intact the herb is, the fresher it will be, so buy as unprocessed as you can and grow your own when possible.

Most leafy herbs are sold as dried cut and sifted, which means the leaves were sliced into small squares and dried, then sifted to remove small stems. I prefer white sage as tips from the ends of stems, creating tight bundles that make for a terrific insta-smudge.

Bark and wood are sold as chunks or shreds. Resins are sold as pearls or pellets. All also come ground into a powder.

If you cannot find a good local herb store, or need specialized herbs, search online. Below are some of my sources:

Frontier
www.frontiercoop.com
Wide variety, except for resins, with increasingly more organics. Low prices, but you have to buy large quantities. Fast service. Lined brown-bag packaging.

Lhasa Karnak
www.herb-inc.com
Incredible selection, especially of Chinese and Asian herbs. Flimsy packaging. Phone orders only.

Living Earth
www.livingearthherbs.com
Small, but high quality operation. Passionate about plants. Mostly organically raised herbs, wild herbs are sustainably harvested. Small selection of resins. Discounts for bulk buys.

Monterey Bay Spice Company
www.herbco.com
Good selection and great prices, especially kitchen herbs. Flimsy packaging.

Mountain Rose
www.mountainroseherbs.com
Industry leader, big on quality and care. A botanical wonderland run by plant geeks. Great selection that gets better every day. Mostly organically raised herbs, wild herbs are sustainably harvested. Slow shipping. Excellent thick vinyl ziplock packaging. Discounts for bulk buys.

Scented Mountain
www.scentedmountain.com
Sustainably harvested Japanese aloeswood or agarwood.

Shamans Market
www.shamansmarket.com
South American woods, resins and herbs.

SomaLuna
www.somaluna.com
Hands down the best selection of resins, with loads of little-known ones and multiple varieties of copal, frankincense, myrrh and even benzoin, plus woods. It's orgasmic! Carries some unusual and rare pagan herbs. Good plastic ziplock packaging. Discounts for bulk buys.

Spice House
www.thespicehouse.com
Multiple varieties of great Indian and Middle East spices like black, white and green cardamom. Exotic (to us) varieties of standard spices like black caraway seed called charnuska. And every kind of peppercorn you can imagine. Good plastic ziplock packaging. Discounts for bulk buys.

Starwest Botanicals
www.starwest-botanicals.com
Fairly good selection with an emphasis on organic herbs. Small selection of resins. Carries some unusual and rare pagan herbs. Discounts for bulk buys.

Of course, growing your own in an herb garden is the best way of all. I love taking a deep snort of fresh dill or lavender; the relaxation is so quick and deep.

Weighing & Measuring

Herbs are generally sold by weight, usually ounces, not by volume. Few folks have an accurate scale around the house, so the recipes in this book are given in dry-weight cup measurements as well as by ratio.

Here are some approximate volume-to-dry weight correlations to use when purchasing herbs:

Barks & Woods	1 cup = 2 ounces
Leaves & Flowers	1 cup = 1 ounce
Roots	½ cup = 2.5 ounces
Sap & Resin Powders	¼ cup = 1 ounce
Sap & Resin Chunks	½ cup = 2.5 ounces
Seeds, Buds & Berries	½ cup = 1.5 ounces

These are average conversions. Small leaves such as thyme will settle more densely and weigh more by volume, as will resin-heavy ones like rosemary. Hairy or fluffy leaves don't settle as much and will weigh less. Little flowers like elder will settle, while larger ones such as hops will not.

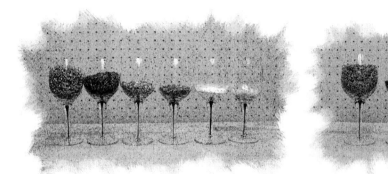

above left: from left to right, an ounce each of flowers, leaves, roots, bark, powder and resin

above right: an ounce of coltsfoot (left) comnpared to an ounce of thyme

Seeds, buds, berries, barks, woods and roots are much heavier than leaves. Saps and resins are the heaviest of all. The same rule applies. Denser, smaller and more finely chopped herbs will weigh more by volume.

Preparing Herbs

When buying herbal equipment, avoid plastic, wood and other materials that absorb aromas.

nesting set of 1, 1/2, 1/3, and 1/4 cups (Yep, they're plastic, but it was the only full set we had to photograph.)

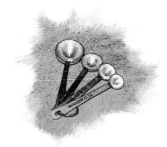

left and right: measuring sets ranging from 1/8 tsp. to 2 tbsp.

Measuring

For making these herb recipes you'll need cups used to measure dry things. (Glass cups are used for liquids.) They usually come as a nesting set of 1, 1/2, 1/3, and 1/4 cups. Look for sets that also have 1/8 cup, which is two tablespoons. You'll also need a nesting set of measuring spoons in 1 tablespoon and 1, 1/2, 1/4 and 1/8 teaspoons.

A scale can be very helpful for people who prefer to work in weights rather than measures. I use a digital postal scale that is accurate to a half ounce. There are much better quality scales out there; I'm just cheap. Folks into precision prefer a triple-beam scale.

digital postal scale

Grinding

Herbal blends need to be a uniform texture so they will burn evenly. Some herbs will have to be ground first, either in an electric grinder, mortar and pestle, or manual chopper. Leaves, seeds and flowers don't usually need grinding unless large, though still, be very careful not to over grind.

small food processor

Wood, bark, root and sometimes saps usually need grinding unless bought as a powder. Gnarlier and harder chunks may require hands-on processing first lest they jam up your grinder. Break such sturdy herbs into smaller pieces by wrapping in a sturdy cotton cloth and whacking away at them with a hammer. Cheesecloth works, but I prefer canvas or one-sided terrycloth. Cloth diapers and napkins also work well. Bark and root can sometimes be cut with large scissors or chopped with a cleaver or large knife – if done carefully!

Almost any food or even coffee bean grinder will do for herbs. A basic pint-sized Cuisinart will do, but I've graduated up to the Cuisinart Spice & Nut Grinder that is specially designed for bulky things. Even so, resins can be hard

on it. Dedicate the grinder to herbs because you'll never get the smell out. After 10 years, my prior Cuisinart became a tannish sage green with an indefinable aroma, like chai tea combined with a garden salad. The electric grinding process kicks up a lot of dried herb dust, so run the kitchen exhaust fan or toss a towel over the grinder when you're working.

mortar and pestle

The classic marble mortar and pestle works for small amounts or softer herbs. Reconstituted stone is preferred since it will not have cracks as natural stone often does. You can occasionally find brass sets. A hand chopper used to mince vegetables can also work for softer herbs.

manual chopper

Blending

Once the herbs have been ground, you'll need a bowl in which to blend them together. Being inert and non-reactive, ceramic or glass bowls are best, but watch for cracks that can fill up with ground herbs. Stainless steel usually works just fine, but it can react with some resins, salts and other substances. Get a big enough metal serving spoon that can both stir the herbs and scoop the blend into its storage containers.

Storing Herbs

Dark and cool are the two key words to remember for storing smudge and offering blends, as well as the bulk herbs used to make them. Sunlight and heat encourage herbs to release their volatile chemicals. I can tell how serious a store is about their herbs by the way they display them. Arrayed on shelves in the front room looks good, but tucked away in a dimly lit back room shows they understand herbs. A dark closet or cabinet is even better for storage.

Humidity is not good for herbs either, so avoid storing in the kitchen and bath, though you can use a humidity-absorbing system like Damp-Rid. Your refrig-

storage jars with a variety lids

erator or especially freezer works great for long-term storage as long as the herb containers are sealed super tight.

Glass containers are the best. It's hard to beat the good old Mason jars, the kind used for home canning. The lid has a rubber gasket that enables you to screw it down tight, and when the rubber gets old you can just buy a new lid. Most large grocery stores will carry Mason jars and supplies. Ceramic canisters keep out light, but I prefer glass jars so I'm able to see what's in there.

Most plastic containers absorb herbal aromas and let in air. If stored in a cool dark closet, industrial vinyl bags like those from Mountain Rose do well for herb storage. If you must go with regular plastic bags, double bag or use dual-lined freezer bags

If you do it right, the blends should stay aromatic and potent for six-months to a year for leaf and flower blends, a year or two for root-based blends, and a few years for resin blends. Bulk unblended herbs will stay fresher a few months longer than blends.

Label everything. I can't function without my Brother labelmaker, found in office supply stores. Write-on labels also work, but try to find water-resistant labels and use a Sharpie or other waterproof pen.

Equipment List

Storage

- double-walled plastic bags
- glass jars
- humidity-absorbing system like Damp-Rid
- labelmaker
- water-resistant labels & waterproof pen

Preparation

- electric grinder
- chopper
- cotton cloth
- hammer
- measuring cups and spoons
- mortar and pestle
- scale

Blending

- ceramic, glass or metal bowl
- non-slotted metal serving spoon

Moonlady's Magical Herbs
A Glossary

Herbs hold such promise and appeal. But it's tough living up to folklore's enthusiastic claims. Below are ceremonial herbs that I remain blissfully in love with, even after all these years. A short treatise on salt and a few nomenclature clarifications rounds things out.

These herb descriptions are highly personal and not intended to be complete. Many excellent herb books and web sites with detailed information exist; one of them will be perfect for your needs. A few of my favorites are listed in **Resources.**

CHAPTER MENU	Ceremonial Herbs
	Rock Salt
	Notes on Male & Female Attributes
	Notes on Planets, Elements & Deities
	Notes on Botanical Names
	Notes on Herb Images

Herbs Glossary

acacia (gum Arabic)
Botanical Name: *Acacia nilotica*
Part of Plant: sap
Aroma: sweet – faintly vanilla
Planetary Ruler: Sun
Element: air
Sexuality: masculine

Qualities: The sap from a spiny shrub or small tree that grows in sandy dry areas is dried and ground to a fine white powder. Some acacias, like those featured in Egyptian myths of immortality, are considered sacred. Gum Arabic adds a very light undertone for blending disparate ingredients in incense. Mix with powders when you want them to cling to something, such as when adding benzoin or dragon's blood powder to resins.

agarwood

Botanical Name: Aquilaria malaccensis, crassna and sinensis
Part of Plant: wood
Aroma: woodsy – with hints of resin and spice

Qualities: More sacred than sandalwood, but far less known outside of Asia, agarwood is also called oud or aloeswood. It has an amazing aroma that can not be synthetically recreated and has no natural analogues. It's able to bring great focus to the mind, placing one firmly in the present moment. Agarwood is over-harvested in the wild. Buy only plantation-raised varieties.

allspice

Botanical Name: *Pimento dioica*
Part of Plant: berry
Aroma: spicy – a blend of cinnamon and nutmeg
Planetary Ruler: Mars
Element: fire
Sexuality: masculine

Qualities: A large berry for a spice, it evokes prosperity.

angelica

Botanical Name: *Angelica archangelica*
Part of Plant: root
Aroma: earthy – slight spice
Planetary Ruler: Sun
Element: fire
Sexuality: masculine

Qualities: A beautiful tall plant with lacy leaves and delicate flowers, the genteel topside belies the root's psychotropic punch. The name refers to the angelic visions it promotes. Medieval Europe's most popular trippy root. Use only occasionally.

angelica

anise

Botanical Name: *Pimpinella anisum*
Part of Plant: seed
Aroma: sharp – anise, licorice
Planetary Ruler: Moon
Element: air
Sexuality: masculine

Qualities: Anise is one of the carminative plants – anise, cumin, dill and fennel – all of which have large umbrella-shaped flower clusters whose seeds absorb gas and generally make the gut feel good. Logic goes that if these seeds absorb the negative inside us, they can do the same outside of us, providing protection on many levels. Anise is an especially happy and versatile plant. Some folks find it makes them frisky, while it provokes visions in others.

asafoetida

Botanical Name: *Ferula foetida*
Part of Plant: root resin
Aroma: foul – garlic gone very bad
Planetary Ruler: Pluto
Element: fire
Sexuality: masculine

Qualities: Toss this powder on hot charcoal and all spirits, malevolent or otherwise, will go away. So will all people and other living things. Asafoetida is extremely foul smelling and should be stored in a disposable plastic container inside a glass jar.

basil

basil

Botanical Name: *Ocymum basilium*
Part of Plant: leaf
Aroma: herbaceous – sharp with strong
     licorice tone
Planetary Ruler: Mars
Element: fire
Sexuality: masculine

Qualities: This favorite seasoning of Italian cooking has a much longer history as a sacred herb, especially in India. Basil is held as a plant of passage though death or initiations where submission is key. There are many different kinds of basil. Use holy basil (Ocymum tenuiflorum or sanctum) when you can find it, often found with Indian cooking supplies as tulasi.

bay laurel

Botanical Name: *Laurus nobilis*
Part of Plant: leaf
Aroma: herbaceous – sharp with a pepper edge
Planetary Ruler: Sun
Element: fire
Sexuality: masculine

Qualities: An herb of honor, prophecy and wisdom, bay laurel clears the mind and enhances stability.

bay laurel

benzoin

Botanical Name: *Styrax benzoin*
Part of Plant: bark resin
Aroma: basalmic – sweet and vanilla-ish
Planetary Ruler: Mars
Element: air
Sexuality: masculine

Qualities: The white balsamic resin from the bark of a variety of Styrax trees clears out old energies and energizes the physical body. It also purifies and focuses the mind. The warm and soothing aroma helps blend multiple aromas.

buchu

Botanical Name: *Barosma betulina*
Part of Plant: leaf, stem
Aroma: herbaceous – bitter, similar to rue with a woodsy edge
Planetary Ruler: Moon
Element: water
Sexuality: feminine

Qualities: A wildly psychotropic and lunar plant, buchu enhances psychic abilities, stimulates prophetic dreams and imparts a touch of the werewolf. (Just kidding about that last one.) This potent plant bears a feminine emotional punch. The smoke is very harsh, but the fresh leaves make a piquant flavoring for brandy and tonics.

calamus

Botanical Name: *Acorus calamus*
Part of Plant: root
Aroma: earthy – musky with ginger tones
Planetary Ruler: Moon (Drew)
Element: water
Sexuality: feminine

Qualities: Also known as sweet flag or sweet sedge, this vigorous aquatic plant is a mild psychedelic with a peppy lift. Many a besotted wanderer has been found waist-deep in marshes chewing this root, which grows worldwide. It inspired some of Walt Whitman's wackier ballads.

calendula (marigold)

Botanical Name: *Calendula officinalis*
Part of Plant: flower petal
Aroma: floral – sharp, a bit acrid
Planetary Ruler: Sun
Element: fire
Sexuality: masculine

calendula

Qualities: Promotes well being and energizes. Sacred to many Mesoamerican goddesses.

camphor

Botanical Name: *Cinnamonum camphora*
Part of Plant: resin
Aroma: resinous – sharp, eucalyptus-like
Planetary Ruler: Moon
Element: water
Sexuality: feminine

Qualities: The aroma of camphor can help bring focus to someone who's overly emotional or libidinous, disassociating, spacing out, or otherwise going over the edge. It's sort of like psychological smelling salts. The essential oil from *Cinnamonum camphora* is more common than bulk camphor, which comes as beige granules. Apply oil to a cotton ball and pass it beneath the nose. Or saturate organic matter with oil, place it on embers and inhale the aroma. Avoid the small camphor tablets used in Hindu temple and wedding poojas, and the camphor found in drugstores. These are made of synthetic camphor that is very nasty, worse than the toxic chemicals in mothballs.

caraway

Botanical Name: *Carum carvi*
Part of Plant: seed
Aroma: sharp – pungent, anise-like
Planetary Ruler: Mercury
Element: air
Sexuality: masculine

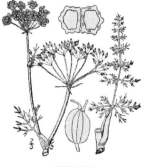

caraway

Qualities: One of the carminatives, caraway contains a lot of aroma and negativity-absorbing power.

cardamom

Botanical Name: *Elettaria cardamomum*
Part of Plant: seed pod, seed
Aroma: spicy – sweet and a bit pungent
Planetary Ruler: Venus
Element: water
Sexuality: feminine

Qualities: The aroma of cardamom inspires not lust but love in men and women. Makes everything mellow. For an aphrodisiac effect, toss some seeds or pods in your hot chocolate, coffee or tea. The pod is best for burning and potpourri. Use the seed for strewing.

cedar

Botanical Name: *Cedrus spp.*
Part of Plant: wood, stem tips
Aroma: evergreen – sharp and resiny
Planetary Ruler: Sun
Element: fire
Sexuality: masculine

Qualities: Whatever continent is grows on, cedar is considered purifying and prayerful. Not to be confused with eastern red cedar, common in the U.S., which is a type of juniper.

chamomile, common

Botanical Name: *Anthemis nobilis*
Part of Plant: flower
Aroma: floral – blend of light apple and clover
Planetary Ruler: Sun
Element: water
Sexuality: feminine

Qualities: Chamomile is like the charming, refined Southern woman who can hog-tie you in ten-seconds flat. It's a sweet, small yellow flower that smells like a meadow, yet nothing's its equal for counteracting the previous negative charge of a space. Walked upon it's very relaxing to the feet.

chamomile

cinnamon

Botanical Name: *Cinnamomum zeylanicum*
Part of Plant: bark
Aroma: spicy – warm, sweet, slightly sharp
Planetary Ruler: Mercury
Element: fire
Sexuality: masculine

Qualities: A culinary plant with a magical pedigree, cinnamon boasts a fiery taste and provides an avenue to spirit and higher consciousness.

clove

Botanical Name: *Syzygium Icimaticum*
Part of Plant: bud
Aroma: spicy – hot, sharp
Planetary Ruler: Uranus
Element: fire
Sexuality: masculine

Qualities: This is the spiciest of the spices and fiery as well. Clove pierces the mind, enabling memories to arise, imprint or release. Like many spices, it's also associated with prosperity.

coltsfoot

Botanical Name: *Tussilago farfara*
Part of Plant: leaf
Aroma: herbaceous – warm, vanilla, mildly
        spicy
Planetary Ruler: Venus
Element: water
Sexuality: feminine

Qualities: When used as a tea, candy or smoke, coltsfoot can counter coughs and encourage tranquility.

coltsfoot

copal

Botanical Name: *Bursera odorata* (Drew), but also other diverse plant
    sources
Part of Plant: resin
Aroma: sweet – warm and resinous with a slight spicy fruitiness
Planetary Ruler: Sun
Element: fire
Sexuality: masculine

Qualities: While trees that produce copal are grown worldwide, the
resin is most popular in Mesoamerica, Central and South America and
serves as a New World frankincense. The pale yellow resin is burned
in ceremonies as food for deities. Though it is masculine in nature, its
aroma can stimulate strong emotions.

coriander

Botanical Name: *Coriandrum sativum*
Part of Plant: seed
Aroma: sharp – licorice-like with a green edge
Planetary Ruler: Mars, Moon
Element: fire
Sexuality: masculine

Qualities: Coriander promotes pleasantness in
all unions.

coriander

corn

Botanical Name: *Zea mays*
Part of Plant: kernel, silk
Aroma: cereal – mild
Planetary Ruler: Venus (Drew)
Element: earth
Sexuality: feminine

Qualities: Corn Mother's gift to North
America remains the culinary staple of many
cultures. It is the offering that best captures
the New World's continental Earth spirit.
Strewing with the various colors of cornmeal

corn

– including yellow, red and blue – can be an art form. Buy organic corn
meal, of course. Use a heavier application to outline sacred areas such
as altars, however, for that you might consider inexpensive horticultural
cornmeal available at nurseries (which won't be organic). Corn silk

represents the maiden and fertility aspects of corn. It comes in a wild tangle of fibers that are a challenge to blend.

cypress

Botanical Name: *Cupressus sempervirens*
Part of Plant: wood
Aroma: resinous – evergreen a bit woody
Planetary Ruler: Saturn, Neptune
Element: earth
Sexuality: feminine

Qualities: The evergreen Mediterranean cypress has been a sacred symbol of immortality, from ancient Egyptian coffins to the Christian cross. It's a long lived tree that is resistant to decay and fire. Unlike most evergreens, it possesses a feminine earth energy, rather than fire or air. Cupressus is the most widely distributed conifer family, so local varieties abound. For the blends in this book stick with Mediterranean cypress, which is commonly available as an essential oil.

damiana

Botanical Name: *Turnera aphrodisiaca*
Part of Plant: leaf
Aroma: herbaceous – sweet, musky
Planetary Ruler: Pluto
Element: fire
Sexuality: masculine

Qualities: With a plant named damiana, you know it's a little devilish, or at least naughty. Indeed, this Mexican herb is known to inspire lust in women and visions in both sexes. Look for damiana liqueur sold in a bottle shaped like a pregnant woman, a traditional and not-so-subtle hint from a mother-in-law to her son's new bride to get busy making grandchildren. Or create your own liqueur by soaking damania in vodka and blending with honey and spices.

dandelion leaf

Botanical Name: *Taraxacum officinale*
Part of Plant: leaf
Aroma: herbaceous – a touch bitter
Planetary Ruler: Jupiter
Element: air
Sexuality: masculine

Qualities: Dandelion seems perfectly designed to channel and disperse spiritual energies of the Earth. A floret of broad, succulent leaves gathers and funnels rain and dew into the thick, deep taproot, while its ball of delicate flowers disperses with the slightest breeze. Fresh leaves are eaten in salads and dried leaves bring a fairy energy to herb blends.

dandelion root

Botanical Name: *Taraxacum officinale*
Part of Plant: root
Aroma: earthy – woodsy with a warm
      edge
Planetary Ruler: Jupiter
Element: air
Sexuality: masculine

dandelion

Qualities: The roasted root of dandelion can serve as a coffee alternative with a grounding energy. Burned, it's slightly visionary and has a roasty aroma.

dill

Botanical Name: *Anethum graveolens*
Part of Plant: leaf, seed
Aroma: sharp – mildly pungent
Planetary Ruler: Mercury
Element: fire
Sexuality: masculine

Qualities: One of the carminative seeds, dill is cleansing and uplifting, yet the seeds make some folks frisky. The aroma of fresh leaves can induce sleepiness.

dill

Dittany of Crete (hop marjoram)

Botanical Name: *Origanum dictamnus*
Part of Plant: leaf
Aroma: sharp – oregano-like
Planetary Ruler: Venus
Element: water
Sexuality: feminine

Qualities: Although Dittany of Crete looks and smells like a typical garden herb, it has a greater

Dittany of Crete

reputation. The smoke aids in the manifestation of disembodied spirits. Inhaled, it assists in astral projection. Keep fumitory or asafoetida on hand, however, just in case the spirits you manifest are not the kind you thought you were inviting.

dragon's blood

Botanical Name: *Daemomorops draco*
Part of Plant: resin
Aroma: resinous – a bit acrid
Planetary Ruler: Mars, Pluto
Element: fire
Sexuality: masculine

Qualities: The resin of a palm tree, dragon's blood usually comes in hard, dense, red clumps that are difficult to measure in quantities unless ground. It adds a potency and sense of action to blends and is associated with empowered dying.

elder, black

Botanical Name: *Sambucus nigra*
Part of Plant: flower, wood
Aroma: floral – with a honey edge; woody
     – with a pleasant sharpness
Planetary Ruler: Venus
Element: water
Sexuality: feminine

elder

Qualities: The elder tree has a great magical history. It brings protection, insight and initiation.

fennel

Botanical Name: *Foeniculum vulgare*
Part of Plant: seed
Aroma: sharp – pungent, spicy
Planetary Ruler: Mercury
Element: fire
Sexuality: masculine

Qualities: This is another of the carminative seeds that absorb negativity. Fennel helps instill courage and action and it has an attractive crescent shape with grooves.

fennel

frankincense

Botanical Name: *Boswellia thurifera*
Part of Plant: resin
Aroma: resinous – light with a touch of spice and sweet
Planetary Ruler: Sun
Element: fire
Sexuality: masculine

Qualities: Frankincense is the classic offering with a light, lovely smoke that represents the Sun and human intellect. The aroma sharpens intellectual perception while it lifts us out of linear thought. Inhaled, it deepens the breath and taken in before bedtime it stimulates dreams. The attractive gold resin is also called olibanum, from the Arabic "al-luban."

fumitory

Botanical Name: *Fumaria officinalis*
Part of Plant: leaf
Aroma: herbaceous – mild
Planetary Ruler: Saturn
Element: earth
Sexuality: feminine

fumitory

Qualities: Fumitory dispels negative energy with a swift kick in the rear, leaving positive spiritual energies mostly intact. It's also good for calming down groups who get cranky and mutinous.

galangal

Botanical Name: *Alpinia officinalum*
Part of Plant: root
Aroma: earthy – ginger with an evergreen edge
Planetary Ruler: Mars
Element: fire
Sexuality: masculine

Qualities: This Southeast Asian root shows up in Thai cooking, psychotropic beverages and Pink Floyd songs. Inhaled or drunk, it stimulates psychedelic visions and lust, which are amplified if the root is soaked in vodka first. A potent dose is useful in breaking old patterns. The leaves have a slight citrus aroma with a strange soapy overtone. Exercise prudence after ingesting this herb. Not for pregnant women or for those under 18.

halmaddi resin

Botanical Name: *Ailanthus malabarica*
Part of Plant: resin
Aroma: floral — like a light gardenia

Qualities: *Ailanthus malabarica* is a sacred tree of India, China and
Southeast Asia, and its grey seimi-liquid resin is essential to nag champa
incense. It imparts the aroma of plumeria flowers, called chamapa in
India. But the tree is over-harvested and the resin increasingly hard to
find. Even nag champa contains ever smaller amounts of halmaddi.

hops

Botanical Name: *Humulus lupulus*
Part of Plant: flower
Aroma: herbaceous — slightly sour
Planetary Ruler: Pluto
Element: air
Sexuality: masculine

Qualities: Hops is a happy vining plant
that makes loads of pale green fluffy
flowers known for giving beer its bite.
Relaxing to inhale, it's a must in sleep
pillows and is also healing to the feet.

hops

horehound

Botanical Name: *Marrubium vulgare*
Part of Plant: leaf
Aroma: herbaceous — spicy, a touch licorice
Planetary Ruler: Mercury
Element: air
Sexuality: masculine

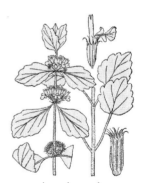

Qualities: When it's fresh, horehound makes
terrific candy. The mucilage-rich tea and smoke
loosens chest congestion and soothes frayed
lung tissue.

horehound

hyssop

Botanical Name: *Hyssopus officinalis*
Part of Plant: leaf, flower
Aroma: herbaceous — strong, slightly bitter
Planetary Ruler: Jupiter

Element: fire
Sexuality: masculine

Qualities: Hyssop is a powerful temple herb renowned for its ability to strongly purge negativity. Inhaled, it stimulates deep breathing. Purifying to the max, it can even engender sadness at the loss of so much held energy. Taken internally, it'll purge you for sure.

hyssop

juniper

Botanical Name: *Juniperus communis*
Part of Plant: berry, wood
Aroma: resinous – sharp, evergreen
Planetary Ruler: Sun (Drew)
Element: fire
Sexuality: masculine

Qualities: Juniper gives us the classic uplifting evergreen aroma, analogous to cedar, that perfectly captures the element of fire and the energy of the Sun. It's used in the recipes in this book as a berry or an essential oil from the wood.

juniper

kava kava

Botanical Name: *Piper methysticum*
Part of Plant: root
Aroma: earthy – woodsy with pepper bite
Planetary Ruler: Venus, Pluto
Element: water
Sexuality: feminine

Qualities: This mildly hypnotic "mystic pepper" makes us tranquil and keeps us alert at the same time. It eases anxiety and promotes insights. In higher doses it encourages psychedelic visions and lust. In Pacifica it is served as a tea relaxant, though some folks like me find the taste quite awful. Kava kava's psychedelic effect becomes stronger if it's prepared with a saturated fat, so make a chocolate milk shake or add a dollop of coconut oil. Do not use it daily. Exercise prudence after ingesting this herb. Not for pregnant women or those under 18.

lavender

Botanical Name: *Lavendula officinale*
Part of Plant: flower
Aroma: floral – herbal
Planetary Ruler: Mercury
Element: air
Sexuality: masculine

lavender

Qualities: Lavender is the herb of romance and happiness.

lungwort

Botanical Name: *Sticta pulmonaria* (Frontier Herbs)
Part of Plant: leaf
Aroma: herbaceous – mild
Planetary Ruler: unknown
Element: unknown
Sexuality: unknown

Qualities: Lungwort is all-around helpful to the lungs.

mandrake

Botanical Name: *Atropa mandragora*
Part of Plant: root
Aroma: earthy – a bit putrid, especially when fresh or dampened
Planetary Ruler: Mercury, Uranus, Pluto
Element: fire
Sexuality: masculine

Qualities: Mandrake is powerful psychic plant that induces a deeply meditative state and enhances vivid dream images. It is a central nervous system depressant and should be used with caution and only in small amounts. Not for pregnant women or those under 18.

mugwort

Botanical Name: *Artemisia vulgaris*
Part of Plant: leaf
Aroma: herbaceous – musty, slightly sharp
Planetary Ruler: Moon, Venus, Neptune (Martin, Drew, Beyerl)
Element: earth
Sexuality: feminine

Qualities: This herb of the Moon is my favorite plant, of course. Even if many herbal experts don't view it as lunar, much of the public, especially female, associate it with the moon. I've watched it turn the silvery undersides of its leaves up toward the Moon and follow it across the sky through the night. Used in acupuncture as moxibustion, mugwort draws energy up and out like the Moon moves the tides. A moxibustion roll, available at Traditional Chinese Medicine outlets, is an easy way to burn mugwort. (It looks like a giant joint!) Inhaled, mugwort enhances psychic abilities and causes prophetic

mugwort

dreams. As a member of the Artemisia plant family, which includes the wormwood of absinthe fame, mugwort should not be partaken of by pregnant or nursing women.

muira pauma

Botanical Name: *Liriosma ovata*
Part of Plant: wood
Aroma: earthy – woodsy, slightly acrid
Planetary Ruler: unknown
Element: unknown
Sexuality: unknown

Qualities: A small Brazilian tree, this frisky plant is stimulating to the libido and the central nervous system and greatly increases skin sensitivity. Often called "potency wood," it's especially effective on men. Soak it in vodka for a love cocktail; add chocolate or coffee liqueur to cover the sharp woody taste.

mullein, great

Botanical Name: *Verbascum thapsus*
Part of Plant: leaf
Aroma: herbaceous – a bit musty
Planetary Ruler: Saturn
Element: fire
Sexuality: Feminine

Qualities: A very fuzzy plant, mullein is high in mucilage and soothing to the lungs.

mullein

myrrh

Botanical Name: *Commiphora myrrha*
Part of Plant: resin

Aroma: sweet – strongly musky with a hint of bitter
Planetary Ruler: Moon
Element: water
Sexuality: feminine

Qualities: Myrrh overrides intellectual analysis and taps into deep feelings. I've seen people burst into tears upon smelling it. It has a most fascinating way of expanding when burned, producing volumes of extremely lively, turbulent smoke that spiritual entities are deeply drawn to. It is purifying and healing, an excellent and often overlooked smudge and an extremely heartfelt offering. Myrrh empowers other herbs when combined with them and provides a lush low aroma note to resin blends. All this richness of spirit comes from a spiny knotted shrub from the Arabia and Africa deserts.

palo santo

Botanical Name: *Burserea graveolens*
Part of Plant: wood
Aroma: woodsy – sharply resinous
Planetary Ruler: Jupiter
Element: air

Qualities: Palo Santo, or holy wood, was used by the Incas for purification and cleansing. It continues to be important to shamanic ceremonies.

passionflower

Botanical Name: *Passiflora incarnata*
Part of Plant: leaf
Aroma: herbaceous – mild, slightly fruity
Planetary Ruler: Venus
Element: water
Sexuality: female

Qualities: Calming and able to promote pleasant communication.

passionflower

patchouli

Botanical Name: *Pogostemon patchouli*
Part of Plant: leaf
Aroma: herbaceous – warm, sweet and musky with slight spice
Planetary Ruler: Pluto

Element: earth
Sexuality: feminine

Qualities: Renowned for inspiring thoughts of romance, patchouli doubles as a prosperity aid. The love and money herb also promotes relaxation of inhibitions and expectations. Its musky aroma adds a warm undertone in blends.

pennyroyal

Botanical Name: *Mentha pulegium*
Part of Plant: leaf
Aroma: sharp – minty
Planetary Ruler: Mars (Drew)
Element: fire
Sexuality: masculine

Qualities: Pennyroyal is not only stimulating and strengthening to the feet when walked upon, it also strongly discourages bugs. Not to be inhaled or ingested by pregnant women.

pepper

Botanical Name: *Piper nigrum*
Part of Plant: berry
Aroma: spicy – sharp, hot
Planetary Ruler: Mars (Drew)
Element: fire
Sexuality: masculine

Qualities: Pepper absorbs negativity and purifies while strengthening and sharpening other herbs it's blended with. It comes in pink, white and black.

pleurisy root

Botanical Name: *Asclepias tuberose* (Frontier Herbs)
Part of Plant: root
Aroma: earthy – mild
Planetary Ruler: unknown
Element: unknown
Sexuality: unknown

Qualities: Another herb that is nurturing and soothing to the lungs.

poplar (Balm of Gilead)

Botanical Name: *Commiphora opobalsamum*,
in US *Populus balsamifera*
Part of Plant: bud
Aroma: basalmic – sharp, resinous, minty
Planetary Ruler: Venus
Element: water
Sexuality: feminine

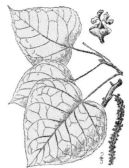
poplar

Qualities: The sap of the rare *Commiphora opobalsamum* tree is the famed Biblical Balm of Gilead's active ingredient. Because it's seldom exported from the Middle East, in the U.S., the resin is extracted from poplar tree buds. Among its more magical attributes is assisting the spirit's release from the body after death. It has a dense, sharp, slightly sweet smell that many entities find appealing.

rose

Botanical Name: *Rosa spp.*
Part of Plant: bud, flower
Aroma: floral – clear, fresh
Planetary Ruler: Moon or Venus, usually
Element: water
Sexuality: female

Qualities: Promotes love and positive feelings, opens the heart.

rose

rosemary

Botanical Name: *Rosmarinus officinalis*
Part of Plant: leaf
Aroma: herbaceous – sharp, resinous
Planetary Ruler: Sun
Element: fire
Sexuality: masculine

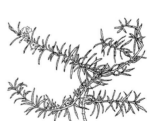
rosemary

Qualities: A resinous purifier similar to sage, rosemary goes a step further to sharpen the mind, heighten memory and encourage compassionate love.

sage, clary

Botanical Name: *Salvia sclarea*
Part of Plant: leaf

Aroma: herbaceous – sweet, sharp and floral
        at the same time
Planetary Ruler: Mercury (Drew)
Element: air
Sexuality: masculine

Qualities: The essential oil of clary sage
promotes feelings of euphoria and
confidence in one's intuition.

clary sage

sage, white

Botanical Name: *Salvia apiana* (Frontier Herbs)
Part of Plant: leaf
Aroma: herbaceous – sharp, herbal
Planetary Ruler: Venus
Element: earth
Sexuality: feminine

Qualities: Sage's botanical name, salvia, comes
from the Latin salvere, meaning "to be saved,"
which reveals the genre's reputation as sacred
herbs. White sage is native to the southwestern
U.S. and northwestern Mexico. Why it's
assigned as feminine and connected to Venus,

white sage

though, I haven't a clue, as it acts totally masculine solar to me. Its pale
smoke is strongly vertical, ascending directly and quickly almost straight
up in a column. The smudge is intensely purifying, sometimes so much
as to leave the aura vulnerable. White sage that grows wild is rarely as
high quality or even the same plant as that grown by herb farmers.

sandalwood

Botanical Name: *Santalum album*, now endangered, and *Santalum
        ellipticum*
Part of Plant: wood
Aroma: woody – spicy with warm undertones
Planetary Ruler: Moon (Drew)
Element: water
Sexuality: feminine

Qualities: A tree of East Asia, ground sandalwood is a staple of Hindu
temple incense. Yellow sandalwood has a softer, deeper smell than the
red, but they look great blended together and a bit of red brings out
the sweetness of the yellow. The warm and slightly resinous aroma

blends disparate aromas together. The smoke is protective and purifying, while the aroma sharpens the mind. It can be used with tree resins to tone down the sweetness. Inhaling the aroma promotes alertness and brings one closer to the divine.

scullcap, Virginian

Botanical Name: *Scutellarias lateriflora*
Part of Plant: leaf, flowers
Aroma: herbaceous – musty, a bit bitter
Planetary Ruler: Saturn, Pluto
Element: water
Sexuality: feminine

scullcap

Qualities: A strongly tranquilizing herb, scullcap works not by sedation but by soothing the nerves. The herbal "chill pill" is a powerful nervine that calms the neurological reactions that fuel anxiety and neurotic behavior.

slippery elm

Botanical Name: *Ulmus fulva*
Part of Plant: inner bark
Aroma: woody – lightly spicy
Planetary Ruler: Saturn
Element: air
Sexuality: feminine.

Qualities: Slippery elm does more than soothe throats with a mucilage-rich tea. It also brings pleasantness to all communication and stops the circulation of gossip.

slippery elm

St. John's wort

Botanical Name: *Hypericum perforatum*
Part of Plant: leaf
Aroma: herbaceous – a bit bitter
Planetary Ruler: Sun
Element: fire
Sexuality: masculine

Qualities: This plant of the Sun boasts yellow flowers that bloom at the height of summer and release red sap when crushed. As a nervine, it soothes and promotes optimism. Inhaled it can cause dreams of a true love or life's path.

St. John's wort

sweet woodruff

Botanical Name: *Asperula odorata*
Part of Plant: leaf
Aroma: herbaceous – with a touch of vanilla
Planetary Ruler: Venus, Mars (Drew)
Element: fire
Sexuality: masculine

Qualities: This gentle woodland herb associated
with Beltane and protection also imparts a
unique flavor to May Wine.

sweet woodruff

thyme

Botanical Name: *Thymus vulgaris*
Part of Plant: leaf
Aroma: herbaceous – sharp,
        lightly resinous
Planetary Ruler: Venus
Element: water
Sexuality: feminine

thyme

Qualities: Thyme is a gentle yet persistent purifier and protector.

valerian

Botanical Name: *Valeriana officinalis*
Part of Plant: root
Aroma: earthy – musty, somewhat fetid
Planetary Ruler: Venus (Drew)
Element: water
Sexuality: feminine

Qualities: Valerian is the original relaxant
that valium imitates in both name and
action. Grounding and stabilizing, it purifies

valerian

and protects. While the foliage and flowers are quite sweet smelling, the
root aroma is worse than old socks, yet cats find it irresistible.

vervain, blue

Botanical Name: *Verbena officinalis*
Part of Plant: leaf
Aroma: herbaceous – grassy, a touch sharp
Planetary Ruler: Venus

Element: earth
Sexuality: feminine

Qualities: The "herb of grace" is like a mellow version of hyssop, just as purifying but not as punishing. It's a mild little plant that boasts a powerful impact and strong protective energy.

vetivert

Botanical Name: *Vetiveria zizanoides*
Part of Plant: root
Aroma: earthy – warm and rich
Planetary Ruler: Venus (Drew)
Element: earth
Sexuality: feminine

blue vervain

Qualities: Another love and money plant, vetivert's earthy aroma is integral to many perfume blends. It's most commonly available as an essential oil.

wild lettuce

Botanical Name: *Lactuca virosa*
Part of Plant: root
Aroma: earthy – strongly sweet, musky
Planetary Ruler: Moon
Element: water
Sexuality: feminine

vetivert

Qualities: Wild lettuce contains a mild opium-like substance that induces a meditative state and enhances vivid dream images. This is a very funky plant, mild on the outside and wild on the inside. Concentrates are widely available on the internet. Exercise prudence after ingesting this herb. Not for those under 18.

wild lettuce

wood betony

Botanical Name: *Betonica officinalis*
Part of Plant: leaf
Aroma: herbaceous – grassy with a musky edge
Planetary Ruler: Venus, Jupiter

Element: fire
Sexuality: masculine

Qualities: Betony has strongly protective and
purifying qualities, plus the interesting ability to
help repair quarrels. A fabulous herb!

yerba mate

Botanical Name: *Ilex paraguayensis*
       (Frontier Herbs)
Part of Plant: leaf
Aroma: herbaceous – grassy with tea-like undertones
Planetary Ruler: unknown
Element: unknown
Sexuality: unknown

wood betony

Qualities: The lusty and stimulating leaf of this South American tree is
the favored herb of Carnival, the mate tea that makes the dancers and
drummers go go go on the streets and in the sheets!

yerba santa

Botanical Name: *Eriodictyon californicum* (Drew)
Part of Plant: leaf
Aroma: herbaceous – strongly musty, a bit resinous
Planetary Ruler: unknown
Element: unknown
Sexuality: unknown

Qualities: An excellent and overlooked herb, yerba santa is one of
my favorites. The Mexican "herb of the saints" is called the "portable
temple" because of its all-purpose ability to purify, protect and provide
a conduit to the divine. It's perfect when paired with white sage.

Rock Salt

salt

Chemical Name: sodium chloride
Aroma: varies
Planetary Ruler: Sun
Element: fire
Sexuality: masculine

Qualities: There is a wonderland of salt in an amazing array of colors and flavors, with sources ranging from seawater to mountains. Conventional table salt is usually made of processed halite. How boring! Epson salt is magnesium sulfate; don't use it for ceremonial salt.

salt

Salt is used indoors to purge negativity and purify. For potpourris, a chunky salt is needed. It will be labeled as chunk, coarse, crystal, grosso or grinder salt. Salt from evaporated seawater is widely available. But seek and ye shall also find coarse pink salt from the Himalayas, brownish pink Hawaiian sea salt rich in volcanic minerals, even sea salt smoked to a deep black.

notes on male & female attributes

In cultural lore, plants are considered to be male or female. Plants that embody strength and active expression, have hot aromas and are dark in appearance, are seen to be male. Female plants are those that encapsulate beauty and receptive expression, have cold aromas and are light colored generally.

Designations for a plant's sexuality mostly agree with those in **A Wiccan Formulary and Herbal** by A.J. Drew. Exceptions are noted and refer to texts or websites in Resources.

Notes on Planets, Elements & Deities

Other cultural assignments include planetary and elemental correspondences, and affinities with certain deities.

In general, air is associated with the east and intellect, ideas and invention. Earth is associated with the north and stability, sustenance and wisdom. Fire is associated with the south and spirit, passion and creativity. Water is associated with the west and emotion, communication and the subconscious.

Planetary correspondences generally match those given by Paul Beyerl in *A Compendium of Herbal Magick*. Exceptions are noted and refer to texts or websites in Resources.

Elemental correspondences mostly agree with those in *A Wiccan Formulary and Herbal* by A.J. Drew. Exceptions are noted and refer to texts or websites in Resources.

Notes on Botanical Names

My source for most botanical names is M. Grieve's *A Modern Herbal*. The specific variant of an herb often makes a great deal of difference. For instance, there are hundreds of acacias, but *Acacia nilotica* is what makes gum Arabic.

Notes on Herb Images

All herb images other than those from QuickArt® are courtesy of USDA, NRCS. 2008. The PLANTS Database (http://plants.usda.gov, 11 March 2008). National Plant Data Center, Baton Rouge, LA 70874-4490 USA.

All Britton & Brown illustrations were scanned by Omnitek, Inc.

angelica
QuickArt® images © Wheeler Arts. All rights reserved. www.wheelerarts.com

basil
QuickArt® images © Wheeler Arts. All rights reserved. www.wheelerarts.com

bay laurel
QuickArt® images © Wheeler Arts. All rights reserved. www.wheelerarts.com

calendula
QuickArt® images © Wheeler Arts. All rights reserved. www.wheelerarts.com

caraway
Britton, N.L., and A. Brown. 1913. An illustrated flora of the northern United States, Canada and the British Possessions. Vol. 2: 659. Courtesy of Kentucky Native Plant Society.

chamomile, common
Britton, N.L., and A. Brown. 1913. An illustrated flora of the northern United States, Canada and the British Possessions. Vol. 3: 517. Courtesy of Kentucky Native Plant Society.

coltsfoot
Britton, N.L., and A. Brown. 1913. An illustrated flora of the northern United States, Canada and the British Possessions. Vol. 3: 531. Courtesy of Kentucky Native Plant Society.

coriander
Britton, N.L., and A. Brown. 1913. An illustrated flora of the northern United States, Canada and the British Possessions. Vol. 2: 647. Courtesy of Kentucky Native Plant Society.

corn
Hitchcock, A.S. (rev. A. Chase). 1950. Manual of the grasses of the United States. USDA Miscellaneous Publication No. 200. Washington, DC. 1950.

dandelion
QuickArt® images © Wheeler Arts. All rights reserved. www.wheelerarts.com

dill
Britton, N.L., and A. Brown. 1913. An illustrated flora of the northern United States, Canada and the British Possessions. Vol. 2: 634. Courtesy of Kentucky Native Plant Society.

Dittany of Crete
QuickArt® images © Wheeler Arts. All rights reserved. www.wheelerarts.com

elder, black
USDA NRCS. Wetland flora: Field office illustrated guide to plant species. USDA Natural Resources Conservation Service. Provided by NRCS National Wetland Team, Fort Worth, TX.

fennel

Britton, N.L., and A. Brown. 1913. An illustrated flora of the northern United States, Canada and the British Possessions. Vol. 2: 643. Courtesy of Kentucky Native Plant Society.

fumitory

Britton, N.L., and A. Brown. 1913. An illustrated flora of the northern United States, Canada and the British Possessions. Vol. 2: 146. Courtesy of Kentucky Native Plant Society.

hops

Britton, N.L., and A. Brown. 1913. An illustrated flora of the northern United States, Canada and the British Possessions. Vol. 1: 633. Courtesy of Kentucky Native Plant Society.

horehound

Britton, N.L., and A. Brown. 1913. An illustrated flora of the northern United States, Canada and the British Possessions. Vol. 3: 110. Courtesy of Kentucky Native Plant Society.

hyssop

Britton, N.L., and A. Brown. 1913. An illustrated flora of the northern United States, Canada and the British Possessions. Vol. 3: 140. Courtesy of Kentucky Native Plant Society.

juniper

Britton, N.L., and A. Brown. 1913. An illustrated flora of the northern United States, Canada and the British Possessions. Vol. 1: 66. Courtesy of Kentucky Native Plant Society.

lavender

QuickArt® images © Wheeler Arts. All rights reserved. www.wheelerarts.com

mugwort

QuickArt® images © Wheeler Arts. All rights reserved. www.wheelerarts.com

mullein, great

Britton, N.L., and A. Brown. 1913. An illustrated flora of the northern United States, Canada and the British Possessions. Vol. 3: 173. Courtesy of Kentucky Native Plant Society.

passionflower
Britton, N.L., and A. Brown. 1913. An illustrated flora of the northern United States, Canada and the British Possessions. Vol. 2: 565. Courtesy of Kentucky Native Plant Society.

poplar
Britton, N.L., and A. Brown. 1913. An illustrated flora of the northern United States, Canada and the British Possessions. Vol. 1: 588. Courtesy of Kentucky Native Plant Society.

rose
QuickArt® images © Wheeler Arts. All rights reserved. www.wheelerarts.com

rosemary
QuickArt® images © Wheeler Arts. All rights reserved. www.wheelerarts.com

sage, clary
Britton, N.L., and A. Brown. 1913. An illustrated flora of the northern United States, Canada and the British Possessions. Vol. 3: 131. Courtesy of Kentucky Native Plant Society.

sage, white
QuickArt® images © Wheeler Arts. All rights reserved. www.wheelerarts.com

scullcap
USDA NRCS. Wetland flora: Field office illustrated guide to plant species. USDA Natural Resources Conservation Service. Provided by NRCS National Wetland Team, Fort Worth, TX.

slippery elm
USDA NRCS. Wetland flora: Field office illustrated guide to plant species. USDA Natural Resources Conservation Service. Provided by NRCS National Wetland Team, Fort Worth, TX.

St. John's wort
Britton, N.L., and A. Brown. 1913. An illustrated flora of the northern United States, Canada and the British Possessions. Vol. 2: 533. Courtesy of Kentucky Native Plant Society.

sweet woodruff
QuickArt® images © Wheeler Arts. All rights reserved. www.wheelerarts.com

thyme
QuickArt® images © Wheeler Arts. All rights reserved. www.wheelerarts.com

valerian
Britton, N.L., and A. Brown. 1913. An illustrated flora of the northern United States, Canada and the British Possessions. Vol. 3: 286. Courtesy of Kentucky Native Plant Society.

vervain, blue
Britton, N.L., and A. Brown. 1913. An illustrated flora of the northern United States, Canada and the British Possessions. Vol. 3: 95. Courtesy of Kentucky Native Plant Society.

vetivert
Hitchcock, A.S. (rev. A. Chase). 1950. Manual of the grasses of the United States. USDA Miscellaneous Publication No. 200. Washington, DC. 1950.

wild lettuce
Britton, N.L., and A. Brown. 1913. An illustrated flora of the northern United States, Canada and the British Possessions. Vol. 3: 318. Courtesy of Kentucky Native Plant Society.

wood betony
Britton, N.L., and A. Brown. 1913. An illustrated flora of the northern United States, Canada and the British Possessions. Vol. 3: 128. Courtesy of Kentucky Native Plant Society

Resources

Books

A Compendium of Herbal Magick
By Paul Beyerl
Publisher: Phoenix Publishing

In this well-organized and lengthy guide to the ceremonial use of herbs, the first section is an overview of herbal methods, the middle section is a fairly concise dictionary of 330 magical herbs with 100 illustrations, and the final section features more information on magical uses of herbs, along with astrological, deity and planetary correspondences.

Cunningham's Encyclopedia of Magical Herbs
by Scott Cunningham
Publisher: Llewellyn

A good book on magical herbs once you parse out the abundant folklore and get to the general qualities of each herb. Features small but helpful drawings.

Magical and Ritual Use of Aphrodisiacs
Magical and Ritual Use of Herbs
Magical and Ritual Use of Perfumes
by Richard Alan Miller
Publisher: Destiny Books

Three excellent books by biochemist and herbalist Richard Alan Miller feature in-depth information on a limited number of very powerful herbs. In addition to tremendous technical details, there's great historical info that is short on folklore and long on verifiable data. Explanations of techniques for herbal preparation and use are drawn from indigenous cultures around the world.

Plants of the Gods
by Richard Evans Schultes & Albert Hoffman
Publisher: Healing Arts Press

Albert Hoffman, the famed inventor of LSD, penned this ethnobotanist's bible about plants that work on the mind with an esteemed biology professor. Contains astounding first-hand information on indigenous cultures around the world with in-depth info on 91 wild herbs, most of which you'll never see in the U.S. Incredible pictures and drawings.

A Wiccan Formulary and Herbal
by A. J. Drew.
Publisher: New Page
An easy-to-use guidebook on herbs covers the full gamut of techniques and contains good info on practical matters like tools. The herbal dictionary is well laid out with surprisingly insightful info, but erratically alphabetized. This great, concise all-around guide is suitable for beginners.

Web Sites

Frontier
www.frontiercoop.com

This herb supplier's web site features an impressive library on herbs. Click on Our Products and then on Herbs (A to Z)

Wikipedia
www.Wikipedia.com

Wikipedia? For herbs? Yep, it's a great source for basic non-magical information, with color pictures, too. Plant geeks have uploaded all kinds of info from primo sources like the USDA database. All entries list their references and contain additional links; some are super-annotated.

A Modern Herbal
www.Botanical.com

Mrs. M. Grieve's "A Modern Herbal" was first published in 1931 and it was indeed modern then. The entire text has been uploaded to a web site in an easy-to-search format. Much more is known of herbs since this book was written, but the author had a discerning eye for ferreting out reputable folklore. Includes good information on plant habitat and growing habits.

Mountain Rose
www.mountainroseherbs.com

Buried in the order page are links for Contemporary Info (worth digging for) and Folklore Info (which is the M. Grieve text).

SaltWorks
www.saltworks.us

The web site of a supplier of gourmet sea salts and bath salts from around the world has a Gourmet Salt Reference Guide that is a fascinating read.

U.S. Department of Agriculture PLANTS database
http://plants.usda.gov/

The federal government is the ultimate source of non-magical plant info. The easiest way to access the database is to click on Fact Sheets & Plant Guides. You can also search by common or botanical name. Much info is available as pdf files. Great pictures!

index of herbs

Book Reviews
&
Readers Respond

Book Reviews

This is exactly the kind of book that I want to see more of—not rehashes of the same old stuff, a bunch of reworked Culpeper and Cunningham. In this book, we get an innovative collection of ideas with enough information to effectively put them into practice, but without a bunch of fluff and filler. In short—this is an awesome book, and I can't recommend it enough.

Lupa
www.greenwolf.com

The reader feels like he or she is having a friendly chat about herbs. Martin's slight sardonic sense of humor entertains the reader on a topic which could be a bit dry. Her directions are easy to follow… tone and style are comfortable and easy to read. Her techniques are unique and convenient for use by nearly anyone. It is obvious she has used the techniques extensively and has put a lot of research and time into this book. Quality shows.

Eileen Troemel
www.FacingNorth.net

I would definitely recommend this book to anyone interested in working with herbs. It is written in a style that is appealing to many different levels of experience.

Dawn Thomas
www. globalgoddess.org/oracle

Readers Respond

I just love Amy's book! I have been a big fan of sacred smudge for years but this tops all! Handfuls of herbs and awesome smoke! Our sacred hibachi has now become a permanent part of our group's Circles!

Bendis ~ Austin

I love your "Spirit Herbs" book. It's really great and so well put together. I was excited to see that you included the information about salt -- so important! The illustrations and pictures are so well done, the charts and recipes are great and easy to use. It's really a joy to work with. I love it! Being able to look up an individual herb in the detailed compendium and finding not only its botanical name and aroma but also its planetary ruler, element and sexuality. The different blends you have created makes this book a breeze to use everyday.

Linda Petty ~ Dallas

After reading Amy Martin's book, I am inspired to prepare herbs myself to create sacred space. Amy's instructions and recipes help the reader to feel comfortable with the processes involved. The book is easy to read, well laid-out and will provide great reference for future ceremonies.

Jennifer Walz ~ Dallas

This is such an informative book, and beautifully formatted and illustrated.

J'Ann Alvarado ~ Irving

A wonderful book. Not just a reference for herbs and their usage, but a work of art, too. What a great addition to my herbal library.

Len Ellis ~ Arlington

8688026R0

Made in the USA
Lexington, KY
22 February 2011